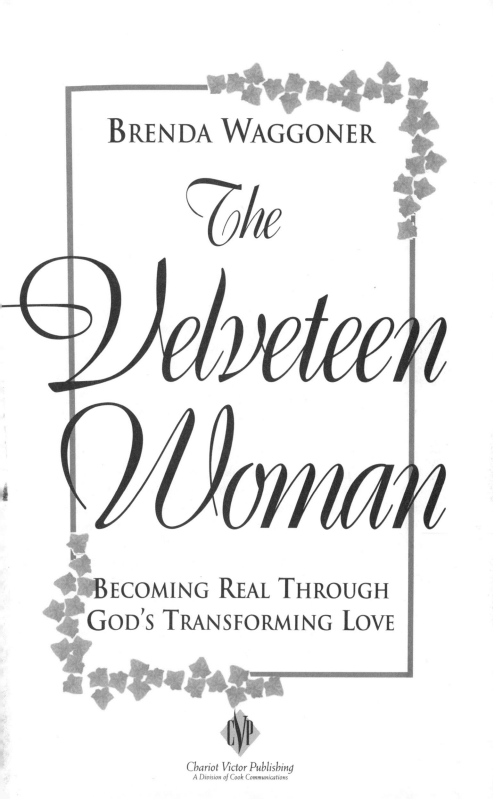

BRENDA WAGGONER

The Velveteen Woman

BECOMING REAL THROUGH
GOD'S TRANSFORMING LOVE

Chariot Victor Publishing
A Division of Cook Communications

"A silky soft fur coat. Many women want one but only a few can afford putting on this luxury. Ironically, taking fur off is even more costly, yet it comes at a price every woman can afford. Sadly, only a few are willing to pay with their lives. My friend Brenda lovingly encourages her readers, unmet friends, that becoming real is worth a lifetime investment. May her hutch increase."

—Gene Getz, Senior Pastor of Fellowship Bible
Church North, Plano, Texas

"What a refreshing book! This is an honest, exciting, and fun book—not about religion, because we've had enough of that. It is a book about a relationship with One whose love never changes. If you want to be 'real,' this book will help. Don't miss it."

—Steve Brown, Author, Professor, and
Bible Teacher for the *Key Life* radio program.

"This powerful, thought-provoking book will touch you deeply. In our image-conscious world, where vulnerability is often in short supply, Brenda Waggoner gives reality lessons for our journey of 'becoming.' Devoid of sugar-coated Christian-ese, Brenda beautifully presents the healing, comfort, and direction we find in the power and simplicity of God's love for us. What can be better than 'snuggling with the Master,' knowing He loves us? I love this book."

—Lindsey O'Connor, Author of *Moms Who Changed the World* and *If Mama Ain't Happy, Ain't Nobody Happy*

With love, to Frank—

*And to all who struggle
to become Real*

Chariot Victor Publishing,
Cook Communications, Colorado Springs, Colorado 80918
Cook Communications, Paris, Ontario
Kingsway Communications, Eastbourne, England

THE VELVETEEN WOMAN
Printed in the United States of America.

Editor: Lee Hough, Becky Freeman
Design: Oh, Wow! Creative

1 2 3 4 5 6 7 8 9 10 Printing/Year 03 02 01 00 99

Library of Congress Cataloging-in-Publication Data

Waggoner, Brenda.
        The velveteen woman:becoming real through God's transforming love/
    Brenda Waggoner.
            p.   cm.
        ISBN   1-56476-748-5
        1. Christian women--Religious life.   2. God--love.   I. Title.
    BV4527.W29   1999   99-25891
    248.8'43--dc21   CIP

Unless otherwise noted, Scripture references are taken from the *Holy Bible, New International Version*®. Copyright © 1973, 1978, 1984 by International Bible Society. Used by permission of Zondervan Publishing House. All rights reserved. Other Scripture references are taken from *The Living Bible* (TLB), © 1971, Tyndale House Publishers, Wheaton, IL 60189. Used by permission; *The New English Bible* (NEB), Copyright © the Delegates of the Oxford University Press and the Syndics of the Cambridge University Press, 1961, 1970. Reprinted by permission; *The Message* (TM), copyright © 1993, 1994, 1995. Used by permission of NavPress Publishing Group; *The New King James Version* (NKJV) © 1979, 1980, 1982, Thomas Nelson, Inc., Publishers.

An effort has been made to obtain permission where necessary for quotations used in this book. Any omissions are unintentional and will be modified in future printings upon notification of the publisher.

Some of the anecdotal illustrations in this book are true to life and are included with the permission of the persons involved. All other stories are composites of real situations with names, places, and details changed to protect confidentiality.

Contents

Foreword

Not long ago I asked my youngest son what he thought of my good friend, Brenda Waggoner.

"I really like her," he said sincerely. Twelve-year-old boys are like those dogs in the movies that can sense real goodness in a person. Kids tend to tell the unedited truth about grown-ups. And Gabe knows what I know, what everyone who meets and loves Brenda knows. There's something amazing about this woman. But what, exactly, is it?

"What do you think it is about Brenda that makes her special?" I asked as I drove along the lake to our home.

"There are too many good things to pick from," Gabe answered.

"You're right." I smiled at my son before turning my gaze out the window. "Too many good things."

Back home in the kitchen I cornered my husband between the counter and the refrigerator and caught him in a hug. "Scott, I want to ask you something."

"Sure," my husband answered, pulling a bar stool up to the counter and taking a seat. "Shoot."

"Okay. We both love Brenda. She's as much your friend as mine, so tell me: what would you say makes her special?"

"She *feels*," my husband replied without hesitation.

I grinned, but immediately grasped Scott's meaning.

"You're exactly right. But I can't just write down 'Brenda feels.' It sounds strange."

"But it's what she does. She feels what others are going through. It's like she's perceptively sensitive . . . "

"Yeah," I mused aloud, "perceptively sensitive."

"And she's open and vulnerable," Scott added.

"And so wise," I said.

"But childlike," Scott countered.

"She's compassionate," I reminded him.

"And passionate about life."

"Yes—and wouldn't you say, 'uninhibited?'"

Scott nodded. "And kind and creative and caring."

"She's just Brenda," I finally said softly.

"She's Brenda," Scott agreed with a what-else-can-we-say? shrug.

As you can tell from the above conversation, it is a rare privilege to be called Brenda's friend. I pen these thoughts on Thanksgiving Day. How appropriate this is, for truly, I am not only blessed with my loving family—I am rich in my friends.

It has been an absolute delight to watch Brenda's work come to life from the conception of the title to its birth as the beautiful, fully grown book you now hold in your hands. As Brenda has written and nurtured and mothered *The Velveteen Woman* over the past year, I've come to feel much like the doting auntie of the project. During its creation, as I read and re-read chapters, I'd often find myself lost in the poignant stories, having to set down my editor's pen to wipe a stray tear off a page. Over and over, I would catch myself thinking, *I know so many people who will love this, who need this!*

Brenda's heart is in every page of this volume. I only wish you, the reader, could have seen the laughter and the tears that graced her face as she poured herself into the writing process. She phoned not long ago, at a point when most writers are ready to fling their manuscripts out the door and be done with it. But not Brenda.

"Becky," she said, "I am sad about almost being finished with this book. I've loved writing it as much as anything I've ever done." That's Brenda—always soaking up joy in the journey. However, this Velveteen Woman can also be a wild hare: there's just enough untamed mischief in Brenda to make her lots of fun.

I've loved many friends over the years, but none have so profoundly affected my life for the better. I believe Brenda has made me a kinder, happier, more loving person just by spending time in her presence. My view of God has taken a subtle shift from the God Out There to the God Up Close as she's demonstrated how to open up to our Father's love. Because Brenda lives what she writes, you will soon get a personal glimpse of her compassionate spirit, as you journey with her to the Land of Real.

You are in for a wonderful, life-altering treat.

Becky Freeman
Author of *Real Magnolias, A View From The Porch Swing, Marriage 9-1-1,* and other books.

Acknowledgments

In appreciation of Margery Williams, author of the well-loved children's classic *The Velveteen Rabbit*, who understood that toys (and people) become Real as they experience enduring love.

Sincere thanks to Lee Hough, product manager at Chariot Victor, for catching the vision of *The Velveteen Woman*, for believing in me as a first-time author, and for so much good help in structuring and guiding this project from start to finish.

Countless men and women have vulnerably shared their stories with me. Their faces have been before me as I wrote this book; their stories often broke my heart and deepened my conviction that God wants to share all of life with us—our joy, sorrow, pain, laughter, and tears—all of it. He wants our hearts. I cannot mention all of their names, and I cannot thank them enough.

Dr. Coyle Stephenson, my pastor, reviewed (several times) this manuscript and offered editorial comments, gave an honest critique, and deepened my sensitivity to the hearts of wounded men and women. Thanks also to Gracie Malone for last-minute help.

My husband, Frank, believed I had something significant to say and went to bed many nights alone so that I could stay up late to finish this book. He walks beside me as we journey toward Real. I am also grateful to have a small part in the life of Frank's son, Brandon.

My sons, Scott and Brent Whitson, have allowed me to share many of their personal stories. They have also taught me so much about loyalty, forgiveness, and what it means to be Real. I love them with all my heart.

Nell Tamillow, my "Texas Mother," prayed countless hours toward the writing of this book. The completion of her journey to Real on September 6, 1998 increases my longing to take my place as the Bride of Christ, and to see Nell once again. I offer thanks to God for all her prayers and love.

I would like to acknowledge Henri J.M. Nouwen, whose books

have profoundly impacted my heart, my life, my counseling ministry, and my writing.

Last, and most of all, thanks to my dear friend, Becky Freeman, for first conceptualizing my own life story as *The Velveteen Woman*, for helping me apply the truths in *The Velveteen Rabbit* to other women's lives, and for naming this book. For lessons in writing and storytelling, for inspiration, encouragement, editing, and agenting. My debt and love for her are equally deep.

Introduction

Most of us are familiar with *The Velveteen Rabbit,* the children's classic by Margery Williams. Perhaps you first heard the story about the velvety bunny while sitting on your mother's lap, or just before getting tucked in with bedtime kisses and good-night hugs.

The story begins on Christmas morning. The Velveteen Rabbit, plush and new, is stuffed inside a Boy's Christmas stocking. The Boy is delighted with his new bunny, and loves him for all of two hours before getting side-tracked by other new toys and gifts. Out of the bright paper wrappings, shiny toys with bells and whistles and fancy clockwork appear. In the holiday excitement, the little Rabbit is set aside on a shelf in the Boy's playroom.

At night, when nursery magic happens, the toys begin to move and talk. Although some of the more expensive toys in the nursery snub the Rabbit, the old and wise Skin Horse is kind to him. One day the Rabbit asks his friend, "What is Real?" The wizened overseer of the nursery, who has seen fads come and go, knows of such mysterious things.

"Real isn't how you are made," replies the Skin Horse. "It's a thing that happens to you. When a child loves you for a long, long time, not just to play with, but REALLY loves you, then you become Real."

The Rabbit asks if it hurts to become Real. "Sometimes," the Skin Horse answers, since he is always truthful. He goes on to explain that becoming Real doesn't often happen to those who break easily or have sharp edges or have to be carefully kept. Bit by bit, the Skin Horse has learned to rest in the transforming love of his master, knowing this is what he was made for.

As women, we will have a myriad of experiences—some pleasant and some painful—as we journey toward Real, to that place of comfortable authenticity with God, with ourselves, and with others. There will be fragile moments of crisis when we feel as though we might break easily, other times when our perfectionism demands we remain "carefully kept." Times when we feel afraid to ask questions, intimidated, confused, or even put on a shelf, forgotten. Through it all, we long to be known, to be loved, to become more Real, but we'd prefer it not take a long time or hurt too much.

The Velveteen Woman is about how the transforming power of God's unconditional love makes us Real. It's a simple story. Just as the little Rabbit became worn and dirty, so do our lives become scarred and stained as we hop—or stumble—down life's varied paths.

But there's hope. Bit by bit, day by day, we can begin to see more of God's pure love for us. To see that His love is unconditional, not based on our outward appearance, our successes or our failures. Though God does not guarantee that all will go well in this life, He does promise to love us always, to comfort us when we're hurt, and hold us close to His heart. He will even redeem our pain, using it to move us toward what Jesus called "The Kingdom of God", or what Margery Williams' timeless classic suggests is the realm of "Real."

Do you yearn to be fully alive, to be known and loved as you truly are? I share your heart's cry. I've had lots of fake "velveteen" fur rubbed off by life, and wandered down many a rabbit trail in search of ultimate love. Now, though I'm a whole lot shabbier and "looser in the joints," I'm finding, bit by bit, deep joy and fulfillment in a more relaxed life with God.

So this book is an invitation from one shabby sojourner to another. An invitation to join me in the arms of our Father's amazing love. To discover what we were made for.

For me, the journey began with a desperate cry. At the time, I wasn't even sure God really existed. It was the first time I ever wondered, *What is Real?*

PART 1

Real Is . . .

A Thing
That Happens
to You

What is Real?
asked the Rabbit one day,
when they were lying side
by side near the nursery fender.

CHAPTER 1

What Is Real?

Dear God, if you're really up there, and if you have the power to make me well, please heal me, I whispered. At twenty-four, I desperately wanted to recover from the mysterious illness that had weakened my body and kept me in bed for more than three months. What would three-year-old Scotty and nine-month-old Brent do without a mommy? And my husband? We'd been married just six years, and all our dreams and family plans lay before us. How would my family survive without me?

Dear God, please! I pleaded. *The doctors don't know what's wrong with me. I'm desperate! If you are real, I beg you to make me well so I can raise my family.*

Amazingly, I began to recover from the strange illness that four medical specialists had been unable to diagnose. Within a few days, I was strong enough to get out of bed, dress, and walk across the street to have coffee with my neighbor, Lillian.

"I think God is healing me," I announced to her, with childlike joy. "I asked Him to make me well, and I think He's doing it!"

"I've been praying for you, too," Lillian responded, with a genuine smile of assurance. "I believe God has a wonderful plan for your life, Brenda."

And so, I began my journey with God. Eager to find out all about this wonderful plan He had for me, off I marched to church, a toddler in each arm and a reluctant husband following about five paces behind. I understood that Jesus had paid a debt I could not pay. I drank up His offer of forgiveness, and charged off to change the world. As the years passed, I thought the Bailey family from *It's A Wonderful Life* had nothing over us, and I smiled continuously, just like Donna Reed. The abundant life appeared ours for the asking.

Until, that is, problems began to dot my perfect life like mud splashes on a shiny new car. Things weren't going well for my husband at work. He grew quiet and withdrawn. Our marriage began showing signs of trouble so, of course, I prayed. And kept on smiling. Then, my husband announced he was leaving home and filing for divorce. The family mosaic shattered. After fifteen years of marriage, my Donna Reed smile cracked into a thousand pain-shaped pieces.

What? God, how can you let this happen? I asked, stunned and confused. *Did you heal me only to see my family fall apart? Was it just a coincidence that I got well? Hello? God? How can this be?* But it wasn't long before I stuffed my honest feelings back into my heart, and plastered a smile back on my face.

Although most of my friends were supportive through the pain-filled process of divorce, a few well-meaning Christians gave me a subtle scolding for daring to ask questions of an all-knowing God. (Didn't I know God was always faithful? Where was my trust in the Lord?) My rising anger felt like blasphemy, so I pushed it down. Instead of facing my real, honest feelings, I resorted to a numbed religiosity, pretending to be strong while I secretly doubted God and His "wonderful plan" for me.

Unknowingly, I'd come to a fork in the rabbit trail. One path led to the "Land of Pretend," the place where everything is neat and tidy, no real problems or pain; the other to the "Land of Real." Not yet understanding the consequences of a make-believe life, I opted for the path of pretending. It would be some time before God would break through my exterior of perfectionism and convince me that what He'd wanted all along was the Real me—doubts, fears, faults, questions, and all.

———— ✦ ————

Today, in my counseling practice, clients often come into my office with armloads of pent-up feelings, similar to the ones I experienced. Just as I was, they are afraid to be honest about their confusion. But once they are assured God can handle their questions, anger, and disappointments, stacks of boxed-up, honest feelings tumble out from behind the doors of their jam-packed emotional closets.

"My two-year-old was killed. I am so angry at God! Where was He when I needed Him?"

"How could a loving God have allowed this sexual abuse?"

"How can life be so messy if God is in control?"

"My husband is having an affair. To lose him in death would have been easier than this agony, this rejection. I am so furious, and there's no one to scream at—just an empty place where my husband once slept next to me."

What Is Real?

How well I remember the day a counselor confronted my own facade of perfection. After my divorce I'd been insisting that I'd forgiven my husband, that I was fine, fine, fine. No anger here. I was only in counseling to get some additional comfort and support. I was a good Christian, and Christians don't get mad, they forgive. I even handed my counselor written proof of my righteousness: prayer journals filled with passages of grief and love, but no anger.

How shocked my face must have looked when the counselor, a strong Christian, leaned toward me and said, "Brenda, I think you are as mad as hell." Shaken, I left his office blinking back tears, daring to wonder, *What is Real? What am I actually thinking and feeling?* But he'd loosened some of the stones in my wall of resistance. The emotions that flowed from that point on were genuine. Painful, yes, but there was a new feeling of peace in being gut-wrenchingly honest. Was I angry? You bet. Was I hurt? To the core. What a relief to let these feelings flow in the safety of a non-judging person and an accepting God. With a bit of new confidence in God's love for me, I took my first step toward becoming Real.

Recently I hosted a get-together with seven women I worked with years ago. As secretaries in a Christian school, we'd raised our kids together and become close friends. Then our children graduated; we went our separate ways and saw each other only occasionally.

Seated comfortably on living room sofas, we began catching up on what had happened in our lives over the last five years. Valerie gave a glowing report about her married daughter, and Jeanette showed pictures of her new grandson. Then all eyes turned to Connie.

"It was hard for me to come tonight," she began, reluctantly. "But since I'm here, I might as well be honest." Sighing deeply, Connie summed up in a single sentence, five years worth of pain and confusion. "My oldest son, Benjamin, quit college, my daughter, Amy, is suicidal, and my marriage is so strained I'm not sure Dan and I will make it." Over the next three hours, Connie bared her broken heart. Still reeling from the intense heartache—a heartache she never anticipated back in the days when our kids shared lockers and lunches at school—Connie felt helpless, abandoned, desperate.

The Velveteen Woman

"I've had lots of questions for God lately. His love is not like I thought," she concluded. As her voice trailed off, I noted a quality of wisdom, even through her sadness, that I hadn't recalled from our conversations in years past.

As our meeting came to a close, we exchanged good-bye hugs and walked out to our cars. Connie and I lingered a few moments, recalling the days when Amy, then six years old, would come to my house to play dress-up, paint, write poems, and sing *Jesus Loves Me*.

"Now I just hope she survives," Connie said with tears brimming, as we gave each other one last hug. As I watched her drive away I felt two conflicting emotions. On the one hand, I was deeply saddened by our melancholy conversation. On the other hand, I felt a great rush of love and a new connection to Connie because of her vulnerability. I hoped that she fully sensed our love for her, without any traces of judgment. I hoped that for a moment Connie might have experienced a lightening of her heavy burden by being Real and allowing us the privilege of sharing her pain.

Connie's questions and confusion brought to mind a conversation I'd recently read about in Sue Monk Kidd's book *When The Heart Waits*. At a conference in Southern California, Sue listened to a minister's wife's eruption of fear and doubt concerning God and faith:

"I can no longer believe in the God I was brought up with," the woman told Sue. "I keep trying to go back to the way it was before. But I only end up pretending. I feel smothered by the lie I'm living, but I'm terrified of what will happen if I face the doubts inside." I think that was the same threshold Connie faced, and me, too.

To be Real, to be authentic, is not always pleasant. It doesn't make sparkling light dinner conversation, and you cannot unmask all your pain with every acquaintance. But those of us who are unwilling to settle for superficial spirituality must learn to be honest with ourselves and with God. And we all need someone with skin on—be it a counselor, a pastor, or a circle of trusted friends—with whom we can open up and be vulnerable.

I'd love to tell you this happens instantly. But every- *What Is* thing worthwhile seems to take time. Becoming Real happens *Real?* slowly, as the Skin Horse so wisely said, "bit by bit." Emily Dickinson once described the sun rising "one ribbon at a time." So do we rise to Real in inches, one day at a time. I wish I could say that being transformed to Real is something altogether in your control, but as the Skin Horse said, "Real is a thing that happens to you."

I hope the insights on the following pages (from many women and men, as well as my own), will assist you on your journey to Real— though it will still seem, at times, painfully slow. In subsequent chapters we will look at some of the road blocks that detour us, and the rabbit trails that distract us from becoming Real. We'll discuss ways to snuggle up to our Master, whether we're in the midst of sorrow, joy, or knee-deep in difficult questions. And finally we'll take a peek into the lives of some women who are becoming Real.

Each chapter begins with a passage from *The Velveteen Rabbit*, and ends with a **Fake Fur Perception** (false beliefs we pick up along the way as we try to earn God's love and avoid pain), and a **Real Skin Reality** (truths about how God really deals with us in life). **Real Skin Realities** encourage us to live life vulnerably, whatever it may bring, in humble dependence on God.

The journey to Real begins with a glimpse of God's love, and it ends with knowing—REALLY knowing—we are loved.

> WE SHALL NOT CEASE FROM EXPLORATION
> AND THE END OF ALL OUR EXPLORING
> WILL BE TO ARRIVE WHERE WE STARTED
> AND KNOW THE PLACE FOR THE FIRST TIME.
>
> T.S. ELIOT

Fake Fur
Perception:

Real is having a neat, tidy-looking theology and Christian life.
By memorizing Scripture and attending church,
we arrive at Real quickly, and without complication.

Real Skin
Reality:

Real is something we become gradually, as we face life vulnerably,
returning to God over and over and finding ourselves loved,
even when life hurts, when it doesn't make sense,
when we're angry or afraid.

Real isn't how you are made. It's a thing that happens to you. When a child loves you for a long, long time, not just to play with, but REALLY loves you, then you become Real.

CHAPTER 2

When He Loves You— Really Loves You

"Jesus loves me, this I know!" shouts two-year-old Jessica, in a loud sing-song voice, as she points her right toe, flings both arms straight up into the air and shuffles across the tile floor. As I watch, I can't decide whether this toddler is performing a ballet or a fencing exhibition. Suddenly Jessica stops her dance as if somebody yelled, "Freeze!", wraps both arms around her shoulders, giving herself a tight hug as she repeats emphatically, "I KNOW Jesus loves me!" My young friend declares—without a trace of doubt or inhibition—the favor that is hers in God's eyes.

What happens to this happy, spontaneous acceptance of God's love as we journey on from early childhood? Perhaps as we gradually learn the depth of our own depravity we lose our confidence. *God couldn't really love me*, we reason, *when I am so judgmental, promiscuous, when I've had an abortion, when I've been divorced . . .*

As we grow up many of us find the years of failure and suffering have made us doubt God. He seems more indifferent than loving. *Does He really know what's happening to me? Does He care?* we wonder. Leaving behind the free-spirited embrace of unconditional acceptance, we try to earn God's love by following rules, pretending to be perfect, hiding our true thoughts, feelings, and pain. Even though God has loved us for a long, long time, it can be difficult to embrace and believe that He *really* loves us, mistakes and all. We may be able to recite the Bible study answers at will. We may know all the verses that deal with His judgment, wrath, and holiness. But what we long for, what we really need is a refresher course on Lesson One: *Jesus Loves Me, This I Know!*

Sherry was in my office for her weekly therapy visit. Life had rubbed her heart raw in spots, and she was trying hard to cover up the wounds. A pastor's wife, Sherry frequently led Bible studies and counseled with women as well as held a full-time job. Lately the demands of pastoring had created an intolerable level of tension between Sherry and her husband. It looked as though they were headed for divorce.

Sherry tried hard to serve God well enough, to do enough work on committees, to lead enough Bible studies, hoping to make up for mistakes she'd made years ago. Her friends knew nothing of her secret past, but her plan to somehow do enough was failing miserably. Not only did she continue to feel guilty, she was exhausted as well.

"There's something I have to tell you about today," Sherry said hesitantly, lowering her eyes.

"Okay, Sherry. What's on your mind?" I asked, trying to make eye contact.

"It's something I'm really ashamed of, but I need to get it out in the open. Before I married Tom, I had an abortion," Sherry confessed bravely, then dissolved into tears. "Actually, it was not one abortion, but three! I feel like such a hypocrite. I am a pastor's wife and I murdered my own babies!" Sherry held her sides and continued to sob deeply, haltingly, as she cried out over and over, "I'm so sorry! Oh God, I'm so sorry!" After several minutes, Sherry wiped the tears from her face and raised her head just enough to look into my eyes.

"Is there any place in heaven for a woman like me?" she asked, eyes filled with shame.

Almost twenty years later, Sherry was still trying to make up for mistakes she made before her marriage. She had done a lot of good things to try to prove her commitment, but good deeds had not erased the painful guilt of her losses. Exhausted and desperate, she simply hoped to somehow gain admission into the back row of heaven. The poet, Louisa Fletcher, has written:

> How I wish that there was
> some wonderful place
> Called the Land of Beginning Again,
> Where all our mistakes
> and all our heartaches
> And all our poor selfish grief
> Could be dropped like
> a shabby old coat at the door
> And never put on again.[1]

In the popular movie *City Slickers*, Mitch, Ed, and Phil, three middle-aged "best buds," go on a two-week cattle drive. Just before leaving, Phil's marriage and life fall completely apart. On the trail, the "City Slickers" take refuge in the tent after a crisis, and Phil's pent-up pain and despair pour out.

"My life is a dead end," he says. "I'm almost forty years old and I've wasted my life." As Phil begins to cry, Mitch reaches out to hug him.

"Oh, Phil." he empathizes. "C'mon, Philly, it's not that bad."

"I'm at a dead end," Phil repeats.

"Yeah, but now you got a chance to start over, you know?" says Mitch. "Remember when we were kids and we'd be playing ball and it would get stuck up in a tree or something, and we'd yell, *Do Over?* Your life is a *Do Over.* You got a clean slate."

Sherry needed to be reminded, as we all do at times, that because of God's love and forgiveness, her life could be a *Do Over.* That she had a clean slate. That God didn't make any back-row seat assignments in heaven.

Perhaps like Phil and Sherry, your life feels like a dead end. Whether you have experienced a divorce, an abortion, the death of a child, the betrayal of a friend, or some other catastrophe, at times all of us need to be reminded that we have a clean slate. In Mitch's words, "You got a chance to start over, you know?"

Though no one can go back and make a new start, anyone can start from now, and make a brand new ending.

Carl Bard, Gloomies

Faith Crisis

Several years after I'd divorced and remarried, the reality of my own life feeling like a dead end grew into monstrous proportions, beyond my capacity to control it. I desperately needed someone to yell, "Do Over."

Standing on the threshold of midlife, I began to question the values and beliefs I'd eagerly clung to during earlier years. In his book *The Ragamuffin Gospel*, Brennan Manning calls this experience a 'faith crisis,' marking "the point at which it would no longer be okay to go on giving lip service to what was not really true for me."[2]

By this time I was remarried to a terrific guy named Frank. But the intimacy I hoped to find on this second try at marriage seemed to be an ever-moving mirage. Each time I reached out for the "wonderful plan" I thought God had for me, I'd once again find my hands filled with the sands of failure and disappointment sifting through my fingers.

Our nest newly emptied, Frank and I moved to the country and began attending a small church, hoping to find some spiritual stability. Before long, though, the pastor reminded me that I had always demanded, as he did, to understand God. I was ripe for his formula to spiritual intimacy, delivered in a neat, tidy A-B-C format. Perhaps this would end the two-year silent treatment I felt I was getting from God.

However, as I would later realize, this particular pastor preached a legalistic obedience that only reinforced my futile attempts to make up for past mistakes. Like small mirrors, the church member's lives reflected their effort to keep the same rules and rituals I'd tried so hard to keep for years, but never quite succeeded. Oh, I felt I'd make it to heaven all right, but resigned myself to accepting that closeness with God was not for strugglers like me who'd been divorced or disappointed their children or battled depression.

At AA meetings, recovering alcoholics use a buzz word, "H.A.L.T.," to remind themselves and each other that if they get hungry, angry, lonely, or tired, they will be especially vulnerable to take a drink. Although my addictions leaned more toward perfectionism and people-pleasing than alcoholism, the AA reminder might have served me well. I was hungry for acceptance, angry at God, lonely in my second marriage, and tired of trying to find a sense of true belongingness in the church. If ever there was a time when I felt like throwing in the spiritual towel, this was it. I'd tried performing, pretending, and perfecting.

Nothing worked. Then something amazing happened.

It was mid-April, and spring was making a slow start in Texas. Shades of green stippled the landscape announcing growth and life to come. The signs of life along the creek side stood in stark contrast to the cold deadness of my soul. I dragged my old wooden rocking chair out onto the back deck to sit in the morning sun. Still cold, I wrapped myself in an old afghan my mother had once crocheted. Rocking back and forth, clutching a little red children's book tightly to my chest, I heard the old wooden rocker creaking and groaning as if to complain under the strain of my weight.

When He Loves You— Really Loves You

Flipping through the pages of the little red storybook I'd treasured since little-girl days, I came to some old favorites. *The Crooked Family. Five Peas in a Pod. The Lost Lamb.* I smiled for the first time in days, as I noticed little smudges of sticky stuff, perhaps tiny chips of a childhood lollipop. And little splashes of hot chocolate. I rubbed my hand over the pages, as if trying to reconnect with something familiar. How I had longed to be held when I was small and lonely. But Mother was usually busy. It was that same little-girl loneliness coming over me again. Here I sat, alone, in the lap of nature. Longing for God's embrace. For some sign that He cared.

"God, You say You love me. I don't feel loved," I declared out loud. If His grace was not true for me, I was ready to know it and stop pretending. "Are you really a *good* God?" I asked. "I want to believe You love me, but the truth is, my sins are more real to me than You are."

As I let my mind carry me back to earlier days, the failures of my past flashed before me as they had so many times before. Like a woman strolling through a memory mall, I window shopped, pausing to stare at a naked little girl sitting in a puddle of childhood shame. A young woman draped in the dingy, dirty sackcloth of divorce. Two little boys, my own sons, in seersucker shorts, trying to smile through tears as their daddy left home because he no longer loved me. Reminders of mistakes. "God, haven't You punished me enough?" I demanded.

It was in this angry, self-condemning state that I weakly called out to God. Clearly, He hadn't responded to tireless spiritual pursuit. Maybe my honest, though angry, heart was more inviting than my usual efforts to impress Him. The truth is, I don't know why God decided to bless me with His presence that day, any more than I understand why He hadn't done it the day before, or the day before that, or the day before that.

It was mid-afternoon when I began to sense His presence, a warmth more intense than the sun's rays. There was no audible voice from heaven, and He didn't visibly appear. I just knew He was there. Like a balm of concentrated forgiveness being massaged directly into my heart, I began to feel comforted, held, blessed.

I closed my eyes, trying to picture how Jesus might look with "skin on." In my mind's eye, Jesus stood before me, and I was aware that I didn't want to look into His face. But the warmth of His presence quickly overcame my impulse to resist. For the first time I could recall, I was looking into the face of Jesus. To my amazement, He was *smiling*. And I realized I hadn't expected Him to smile. Perhaps I thought He'd peer down His nose at me through lenses of legalism, judging my past mistakes as harshly as I judged myself. Instead, He gazed into my eyes with tenderness and compassion such as I'd never seen or felt.

Still rocking, I basked in His loving presence. After a few minutes, thoughts began to come: *Jesus loves me*. Reaching for a spiral notebook and pen, I wrote down: Jesus loves me. The reality of the words on the page began to sink into my heart, as I gratefully returned His gaze. More thoughts came into my mind, and then flowed from pen to paper:

> *I was a lonely little girl . . . and Jesus loved me.*
> *I tried to make my first marriage work, but I didn't know how . . .*
> *and Jesus loved me.*
> *My children suffered pain and loss due, in part, to my actions . . .*
> *and Jesus loved me.*
> *I got angry at God because I didn't get the answers I wanted . . .*
> *and Jesus loved me.*
> *I threw up my hands and admitted failure . . .*
> *and Jesus loved me.*
> *There is hope for my future . . . because Jesus loves me.*

As I closed my eyes again, the shop windows in the mall flashed through my mind for a second time. I strolled through the memories once more. This time I wasn't asking for His approval, just sensing His love. Picturing Jesus walking with me, smiling at me. As we passed by the two sad little boys, Jesus bent down to look into their tear-stained faces. Reaching out His arms, the two boys ran to Him. As He enfolded them in an embrace, tears welled up in His own eyes. Perhaps He understood, more than anyone else could, the agony of separation from His Father.

Then Jesus stood up, walked over to the woman draped in sackcloth. As she stood before Him, eyes downcast, He brushed her cheek lightly with the palm of His hand. Jesus stood before the woman for a long while. Her eyes still would not meet His gaze. He waited. Then, with His hand, He gently raised her chin as if to say, "Look at Me." As her eyes met His, her white mannequin face took on a rosy, lifelike glow. She'd never seen such a depth of genuine tenderness and compassion. His approving smile seemed to convey to her this message: "I love you. I have always loved you. Not for who you think you *should* be, but just because you are mine."

When He Loves You— Really Loves You

Opening my eyes at last, I saw that the leaves on the photinnia bushes now glistened in the pre-sundown glow. I had been in the rocking chair all day. I cried uncontrollably for two days straight, tears flowing from a grateful heart. Never before had I sensed God's presence so strongly.

Although I have asked many times for a duplicate experience, it has not happened. Days of feeling far from God would come again. But something changed forever. For the first time, I believed I was loved— *really* loved—mistakes and all. That day, these words of A.W. Tozer became a reality for me: "God formed us for His pleasure, and so formed us that we as well as He can in divine communion enjoy the sweet and mysterious mingling of kindred personalities. He meant us to see Him and live with Him and draw our life from His smile."[3]

At a time in my life when I deserved it the least, God had come to me to show me His smile. To reveal to me His acceptance and unconditional love. To tell me that no matter how many mistakes I had made, He would never stop loving me. That I could stop trying to understand His love, or deserve it. All I could do was accept it. It was a gift especially for weaklings and doubters and ragamuffins like me.

> YOU HAVE TURNED FOR ME MY MOURNING INTO DANCING.
> YOU HAVE PUT OFF MY SACKCLOTH
> AND CLOTHED ME WITH GLADNESS.
>
> PSALM 30:11 (NKJV)

I don't expect every woman's experience to mimic mine. In fact, I would prefer others not struggle as long as I did, or hold on to their rabbit fur as desperately as I did. But the human spirit is often stubborn and wily, and each woman is likely to face at least one uniquely designed crisis before discovering God's love is based solely on His nature, not her track record.

Of course, we do feel guilt over our sins, but healthy guilt leads us to claim responsibility, feel sorry, and then move on to gratitude, knowing our wrongs have been redeemed. Somehow many of us picked up the idea that holiness is something we can attain if we can just be efficient and quit making so many mistakes. But holiness is not something that can be earned. As Brennan Manning says, "Holiness is not an attainment at all—it's a gift. He sanctifies and does it all. It is never do, do, but be, be and I will do."[4]

Ragamuffin Therapist

GOD IS SAYING TO THE WHOLE WORLD: I LOVE YOU. YOUR SINS ARE FORGIVEN BECAUSE OF THE CROSS.

BILLY GRAHAM[5]

In my role as a therapist, I often have the privilege of watching a woman begin shifting her focus from her own badness to God's goodness; from her mistakes to God's full pardon. Occasionally, there are rare golden moments when it is clear that God is not only at work in redeeming my own ragamuffin past, He's helping me, a wounded healer, give others a taste of His love. Today is such a day.

Lisbeth smiles as she tells me she's been fired from her bartending job because her six-month-old baby has been sick so much. She says she's happy because now she can be with her baby more. But that means her boyfriend has to get a job and keep it! As she gets more comfortable, Lisbeth gradually unfolds the details of a painful chapter in her life story.

She begins by revealing that she once sexually betrayed her first husband, and it has haunted her ever since. She'd like to marry her current boyfriend, but so far they are just "together" because Lisbeth is not sure she has enough to offer him to warrant a permanent commitment. This revelation leads to deeper places where questions about God lurk.

Lisbeth wants to believe in God, she says, but finds it difficult to trust Him. To believe that God is love is one thing, but to believe that He *really* loves *her* is quite another.

"One day," Lisbeth declares reflectively, "a lady from a nearby church said I should say a prayer and receive Jesus. So I repeated the words she told me to say, but had no idea what it meant." A puzzled frown forms in her brow. "I never saw that woman again. What did that prayer mean?" Lisbeth asks.

When He Loves You— Really Loves You

Without waiting for a response from me, Lisbeth goes back to her story about how she hurt her husband, someone she cared about. "He was such a nice guy. How could I do that to him?" she cries out in agony.

I know I'm the therapist, and I'm supposed to act like a professional, but I can't hold my own tears back as I listen to her wailing, gasping for breath. So I ask her to pass the box of Kleenex.

Finally, when it is time for the session to end, I manage to say, "Lisbeth, I'm so glad you're here."

She looks at me tentatively and asks, "So, there must be some hope for me?" I nod, too moved to manage a fuller response. "Thanks for saying that," she whispers. "I'm glad too."

After Lisbeth leaves, I spend a few moments reflecting on this precious ragamuffin who understands so well how sin hurts us. By not forgiving herself for things that happened a decade ago, Lisbeth believes her own self-contempt will keep her in line and prevent her from messing up again. It's a subtle, insidious shame game we play with ourselves. "In a world of ungrace, structured shame has consider-able power. But there is a cost, an incalculable cost: ungrace does not work in a relationship with God."[6]

How *do* we recover from the guilt of self-inflicted losses? Perhaps we can learn a lesson from Brian G., an alcoholic. His past was littered with estranged wives, family, friends, and employers. When asked, "How can you handle the guilt and pain of knowing your failures?" Brian simply answered, "I don't handle it. If I tried, I'd be drunk right now. I face my sin. God handles it. Others may not forgive me, and I may not forgive myself. But this I know—God accepts me, warts and all."[7]

Brian knew that the guilt of his past was more than he could han-dle. So he asked God to do it. He knew that God's love was a gift. A gift so special that it turns mistakes into holiness. A gift that breathes new life into our dead hearts, so we can again see the smile of Jesus, who came for all of us ragamuffins. A gift that makes a woman's heart dance with uninhibited freedom, so that she can once again declare with child-like joy, "Jesus loves me, this I know!"

Fake Fur
Perception:

I can never be loved by God unless I can first figure out
some way to make up for my past mistakes.

Real Skin
Reality:

Jesus died to pay for all of my mistakes.
There's nothing I can do to make Him love me
any more, or any less.

Weeks passed, and the little Rabbit grew very old and shabby, but the Boy loved him just as much. He loved all his whiskers off, and the pink lining to his ears turned grey, and his brown spots faded. He even began to lose his shape, and he scarcely looked like a rabbit any more, except to the Boy.

To him he was always beautiful.

CHAPTER 3

The Gift on Christmas Morning

When my youngest son was about three years old, he and his grandma would play a little game. Brent would begin by asking, "Grandma, why do you love me?" Grandma's reply would always be, "Just because." After a few gleeful giggles, Brent would ask, "But Grandma, *why* do you love me?" And Grandma would again say, this time a bit louder and with a generous smile, "Just because."

Sometimes their dialogue would end there as Brent became distracted by a favorite toy. But just as often, he would persist with his question a third time, as an elflike grin spread across his face in anticipation of what he knew was to come. "But *WHY*, Grandma, *WHY* do you love me?" This time Grandma would stop whatever she was doing to chase down my three-year-old son, tickling his ribs as she repeated over and over, "Because, because, because!"

For Grandma, there was no better explanation for loving her grandson than "just because." In the same way, the Boy didn't need any particular reason to love the Velveteen Rabbit through years of the bunny's losing his shape and sheen. To the Boy, the Rabbit was always beautiful. Just because.

Far surpassing any human models of love, God *really* loves us—just because. Although we may be *feeling* vulnerable, unprotected, and wondering, *How can God be loving me, when my life looks like such a mess?* He carries us, holding us close to His heart.

The Velveteen Woman

Perhaps we can gain some understanding from a few scenes in the popular movie *Forrest Gump*. Near the end of the film, Forrest's lifelong love, Jenny, finally agrees to marry him, after years of rebellious living. Now terminally ill, Jenny returns to their hometown, to Forrest, who had once said to her, "I may not be a smart man, but I know what love is." During the final days of her life, Forrest lovingly cares for her.

One day, as he sits on the side of Jenny's bed entertaining her with tales of his travels and adventures, she says dreamily, wistfully, "Oh Forrest, I wish I had been with you then."

Forrest looks at her in disbelief, puzzled and confused by her musing. "You *were* with me, Jenny," he explains. "I thought about you all the time."

Forrest gives us a touching glimpse of God's loving us without conditions. God is thinking about us all the time, carrying us with Him everywhere He goes. He wouldn't even *consider* leaving us behind. Even at times when it seems to us that we're being stripped of everything precious, left alone to comfort ourselves in whatever ways we can find. Even then, He holds us close to His heart.

O LORD, YOU HAVE SEARCHED ME AND YOU KNOW ME. YOU KNOW WHEN I SIT AND WHEN I RISE; YOU PERCEIVE MY THOUGHTS FROM AFAR. YOU DISCERN MY GOING OUT AND MY LYING DOWN; YOU ARE FAMILIAR WITH ALL MY WAYS.

PSALM 139:1-3

Unconditional Love

When I think of the words *unconditional love*, I am transported to a familiar scene described for us in the Bible about a father and his two sons. The younger son asked for his share of the family inheritance, and the father granted his request. The son then squandered all his money in a faraway country and became destitute. There was a famine in the land, and a farmer hired the son to feed his pigs. Even the husks from the pigs' food looked good to the wayward young man.

Desperate and hungry, the younger son returned home, hoping his father would be generous enough to hire him as a laborer. To the son's utter amazement, his father ran out to welcome him with open arms. The loving father, who never stopped aching for the sight of his son coming up the road, interrupted the boy's well-rehearsed apology to announce that a feast would be prepared in honor of his return. The father did this in spite of protests from his jealous older son.

The Gift on Christmas Morning

In your life, you may have had a much different experience. Perhaps you've done a wayward thing or two yourself, and you weren't met with such a generous welcome when you returned home. The loving father in this story gives us a picture of God we don't often see in human beings. Some prodigals are never welcomed home by their dads, or their churches. At least not so quickly, nor so easily.

Shug Avery, a nightclub floozy in the movie *The Color Purple*, provides us with a poignant look into the heart of just such an unwelcomed prodigal. Turned away by her preacher-dad, Shug looked to other men, trying desperately to find love. Although she pleaded with her father, he repeatedly refused to speak to Shug because of her carousing lifestyle. Years passed. Still her father stood in the pulpit telling others about God, turning his back on Shug, even when she tried to tell him about her recent marriage, hoping this news might make him proud.

Then one Sunday morning, Shug was singing in a nightclub just down the street from her father's church, which happened to be meeting at the same time. During a quiet moment in the nightclub, Shug heard the faraway voices of the church choir singing "God's Tryin' to Tell You Somethin'." Slowly, Shug started to clap to the rhythm of the song she'd no doubt learned as a child. "Oh, yes, Lord," she sang out, echoing the choir as if in response to a heavenly call. Then, clapping and singing the hymn, she walked out of the nightclub, down the road, and into the church, followed by everybody who'd been in the club, clapping and singing.

Down the aisle and right up to the pulpit Shug marched with her rag-tag following of singers. By this time, the church choir was silent, and all eyes were fixed on Shug, including those of her father. "God's Tryin' to Tell You Somethin," she belts out one more time.

At last, he hears.

After years of rejection, at last, her father opens his arms to embrace his love-starved daughter.

We may expect God to respond in the way Shug's preacher-father did for years, turning His back, punishing us with silence. But although God is silent at times, He never rejects any of His children. No matter what condition we are in as we come up the road to return to His arms, to Him, we are always, always beautiful.

During the early years of my spiritual journey, I identified strongly with the prodigal son's older brother, having done my best to be a dutiful daughter and please my parents. My only sister, Jan, married and had a child while she was quite young (*too* young, I thought), and I wanted so much for my parents to notice my achievements and virtuous behavior.

"You're always thinking about her," I self-righteously whined. "She's having nothing but problems, and you're hardly even noticing how well I'm doing."

As the years passed, however, my own life was soon checkered with failure. The story of the Prodigal Son took on new meaning for me as, for the first time, I began to identify with the younger, wayward son. The fact that the father loved him even while he was still in the faraway country took on deeper significance.

I have to admit, there are times when I still identify with the self-righteous older brother, outwardly faultless but inwardly preoccupied with bitterness and jealousy. At other times I am more like the younger son, making visible mistakes that sometimes scar my life. Whether I'm the prodigal, the self-righteous older brother, or somewhere in between, God emphasizes what He most wants me to hear, without ever altering His standards of holiness. "I love you when you succeed, I love you when you fail. I love you when you're good, I love you when you're bad. I love you when you obey me, I love you when you turn your back on me." Though it defies human logic, our Father opens His arms to welcome us home without question, whether our ears are satiny pink with piety, or gray and stained from our latest visit to the pig sty.

It's four days before Christmas, and I'm just now setting up the nativity scene and baking the sugar cookies. But now, I decide it's time to take a break from holiday chores. Wearing my comfy sweats and sipping hot spiced tea, I plop down in my favorite swivel rocker to enjoy the lights on the Christmas tree.

The Gift on Christmas Morning

As Celtic carols play in the background, I am reminded of the pastor's morning sermon, perhaps the most meaningful message I could recall about the infant Jesus coming to earth. Unlike so many Christmas messages I'd heard before, our pastor didn't skip over, but rather centered on the genealogy of Christ. As the pastor began reading through the names, I let out a ho-hum yawn that was almost audible. *Who cares about all those names?* I questioned impatiently. *Let's get on with the story.*

It took a while, but it finally dawned on me: the genealogy *was* the story. The whole story. Matthew's Gospel names four women in the royal line: Tamar, Rahab, Ruth, and Bathsheba, none of whom epitomized what we would expect to find as the relatives of Jesus. Two of the women were prostitutes, one a cursed Moabite, and the other an adulteress.

As the sermon continued, the significance of Christ's family tree became evident. These very names were symbols of God's grace. Because of God's deep desire to *identify* with us, His children, He sent His own sinless Son to earth through a lineage of sinners just like me and you. "John the Baptist preached to sinners . . . but Jesus identified with them. He went out of his way to mix socially with beggars, tax collectors, and prostitutes."[1] He didn't want us to feel alone on this hard-edged planet. Those seventeen verses of genealogy were like neon signs blinking a message God wants each of us to receive: "I'm now one of you! I understand what it is like to wear the skin of a man!"

As a recovering legalist, I admit I cannot fathom the depth of a love so fierce, so far-reaching. A love that concerns itself with our well-being, even when we are faithless. When we fall for the enemy's lies, playing the role of a harlot and betraying God, He stands by, ready and willing to welcome us home. Though we repeatedly refuse to trust Him to take care of us, He endures our unfaithfulness because He simply refuses to stop loving us.

Twisted Lips and Crooked Lives

Brennan Manning, in his grace-laden book, *The Ragamuffin Gospel,* quotes author/surgeon, Richard Selzer, M.D., who describes this poignant scene in a hospital room:

> *I stand by the bed where a young woman lies, her face postoperative, her mouth twisted in palsy, clownish. A tiny twig of the facial nerve has been severed. She will be thus from now on. Her young husband is in the room. He stands on the opposite side of the bed and together they seem to dwell in the evening lamplight, isolated from me, private.*
> *"Will my mouth always be like this?" she asks.*
> *"Yes," I say, "It will. It is because the nerve was cut."*
> *She nods and is silent. But the young man smiles.*
> *"I like it," he says, "It is kind of cute."*
> *Unmindful, he bends to kiss her crooked mouth and I am so close I can see how he twists his own lips to accommodate to hers, to show her that their kiss still works.*[2]

The image of this loving husband twisting his lips to kiss his wife's deformed mouth leaves us with a vivid picture of God's grace. Countless times I have thought God would and should turn away from me in repulsion because of my twisted life. Have you ever had similar thoughts? Do you expect rejection from God when you fail? It stands to reason that we would have difficulty believing He *loves* us even when He can't approve of our behavior. But He does. When we make mistakes, God redeems our flaws and stoops to embrace our humanness.

There were days when I took pride in knowing that at least I was not a prostitute like Rahab or an adulteress like Bathsheba. But life has taught me this kind of smugness is a phony blanket of security. The pink sateen lining of my velveteen ears has turned gray from careless decisions, and my colorful brown spots are fading fast with years. I now see how my perfectionism and judgmental ways have hurt those I love. Yet, in spite of my failure, most everyone in my family still loves me.

My oldest son, Scott, and I are good friends now. It hasn't always been so. There were days after my divorce when I was so busy struggling to survive that I was not emotionally there for him, perhaps when he needed me most. Scott was a young adolescent trying to juggle his own feelings of rejection and the loss of the family he'd always known. If ever there was a time when my son needed a supportive mom, this was it. And I was too weak to help him. In all honesty, as I look back, I see how much I let my son down. Yet somehow, after a few years of maturing and a bit of love-scrubbing from life, Scott forgave my imperfection. He now seems content to share our partially shabby past, along with some newer patches of genuineness. Together, we're becoming more Real, as God's grace is lived out in our unique family tree. To each other, we are beautiful. Not perfect, but beautifully human.

———◆◇—— ——◇◆———

The Gift on Christmas Morning

The Velveteen Rabbit arrived as a gift on Christmas morning. So too, the infant Jesus—God's gift to mankind—was laid in a lowly manger at Christmas. Sent to earth through a lineage of sinners. Given so that we could become Real, so all could know they are loved without limits.

Just as the pink satin lining of the Rabbit's ears turned gray and his brown spots faded, we lose our shape, becoming worn and scarred by life as the years pass. But God loves us just the same. To Him, we are always beautiful. Whether we're clean or dirty, obedient or rebellious, prodigal or self-righteous, or somewhere in between.

Like the soft, golden glow lighting the face of a treetop angel, the royal lineage of the Christ Child shines a holy spotlight on God's grace. Look closely at the packages underneath the tree—that's *your name* written on one of the gift tags. His love is your gift.

He loves you.

Just because.

Fake Fur Perception:

If God's love requires absolutely nothing of me,
it can't be very valuable.
I must earn God's grace through holy behavior.

Real Skin Reality:

Because of God's love, He sent Jesus to bridge the gap between
His holiness and my humanness. I was created to be
intimately loved by Him, "just because."

PART 2

Road Blocks
and
Rabbit Trails

The Skin Horse was wise, for he had seen a long succession of mechanical toys arrive to boast and swagger, and by and by break their mainsprings and pass away, and he knew that they were only toys and would never turn into anything else. Even Timothy, the jointed wooden lion, who was made by the disabled soldiers, and should have had broader views, put on airs and pretended he was connected with Government.

CHAPTER 4

Mechanical Toys and Wind-up People

When my two sons were little boys, their dad and I would often take them to the batting range to hit balls. The pitching was always good, and Scott and Brent didn't have to worry about breaking a window or hitting the ball over the fence. They could concentrate solely on "slugging it."

Since Scott was older, he often got some extra instruction from Dad.

"Choke up on it, son. Don't take your eye off the ball!" In the next batting station, Brent would grow impatient.

"Daddy! Watch me! Daddy! Daddy! WATCH ME!"

"Okay, son," Dad would say, turning his attention to Brent. "Make it a good one!" Here's where the tables turned. Now it was Scott's turn to lose patience, thinking he was not getting his fair share of Dad's attention.

"Watch ME, Daddy! Watch ME!" Scott would shout. "I hit a home run! Daaaaaa-Deeeee! WATCH ME!" (Have you ever noticed that it's not nearly as much fun to make a great hit when nobody's watching?)

I've often wondered if this is not what I sometimes do with God, shouting at Him to watch me make my next grand performance or great hit. If I'm striking out, of course, I'd prefer He just look the other way.

But if I'm working hard on my game, I want to be sure He's looking. *Father, watch me! You don't want to miss this one! I sure hope You appreciate this! Did You see how well I did that? Watch me!* Without a hint of the childlike vulnerability my sons seemed to have, I boast and swagger like a mechanical toy wound up tight, ready to make an impressive debut.

When we are young children, our homes provide the first natural stage, and feature our parents as performance directors. Then, we grow into adults and the world becomes our stage. We play our grown-up roles before an audience of fellow human beings. As Jacques said in Shakespeare's *As You Like It*, "All the world's a stage, and all the men and women merely players."

Though we'd prefer to think we're following God's direction, too often we allow others to write our scripts and direct our steps. For most of us, it takes years before we transfer our trust from parents and significant others to God. Meanwhile, instead of spontaneously shouting, "Watch me!" with childlike enthusiasm, adults often turn to more sophisticated acting techniques. We may just trick ourselves into thinking we're performing perfectly at all times. Unaware, all the while, that all our Director really wants is our love and tears, frustration and smiles—our honest, spontaneous responses to the dramas of life.

MUCH OF THE VAST NETWORK OF CHRISTIAN ACTIVITY AND SERVICE IS BENT ON PROPAGATING AN ANSWER FOR PEOPLE'S NEEDS AND PROBLEMS WHICH FEW OF THOSE PROPAGATING IT ARE FINDING ADEQUATE IN THEIR OWN LIVES.

ROY AND REVEL HESSION[1]

Rita's sixteen-year-old daughter was having health problems. She'd suffered mild headaches for over a year, and now the pain was getting worse. To top it off, she'd begun sleeping much more than usual—at least twelve hours a day. After taking her daughter for evaluation by a general practitioner, a neurologist, and an internist, Rita was growing weary.

"How are *you* doing?" I asked Rita one day when I called on the phone.

"Oh, I'm fine. I'm sure God has this all under control, and it will all turn out," she replied flatly. Rita recited her lines well. It took about thirty minutes of small talk before I sensed her fragile but firm spiritual facade softening.

"Let me ask you again, Rita, how are you doing?"

"I know, I'm supposed to trust the Lord. And God knows I'm trying. But the truth is, I'm scared to death! Sometimes I just wish the doctors would tell me if my daughter is going to die. This uncertainty is so frightening!"

Mechanical Toys and Wind-up People

Rita went on to explain, reluctantly at first, that friends didn't really want to hear about her confusion, fear, even panic. That they seemed disappointed in her if she didn't "have faith," and then Rita felt guilty. So she'd decided to follow the "religiously correct" script and say she was just fine.

The church had become Rita's stage. As she played out a performance before an audience of religious friends whose applause she sought, the voice of her Master Director grew faint. Distant. John Powell says that in our search for acceptance and approval from others, "we have been somehow *programmed* not to accept certain emotions as part of us. We are ashamed of them."[2]

Although it doesn't seem to be true, we actually move further away from God when we act with practiced precision a religion of denial, concentrating all our effort on *not making mistakes*. Perfection becomes our god. And for a while, it may appear to work beautifully. It feels right because we're in control. Have you ever struggled to perform perfectly to earn approval and love? When we serve the god of perfection, we are internally programmed by fear. We say and do all the "religiously correct" things, like Christian mechanical robots. Instead of admitting our genuine, unruly emotions and letting our bruised spots show, we are quick to declare that we're "turning things over to God," covering up our Real emotions with religious layers of phoniness. Unaware, all the while, that "perfectionism, in a Christian sense, means becoming mature enough to give ourselves to others."[3] Relaxing and letting our Real skin show.

Are you aware of a time when you pushed God away and rejected your honest emotions in favor of looking strong? I can recall many such times as I look back over my life. They were lonely hours. Empty, barren times of self-betrayal . . .

*What am I doing
in this lonesome chamber,
looking so strong,
feeling so weak.
Why did I come?*

*What consolation
did I hope to find
in this empty room
with unspoken needs;
my self betrayed?*

*Why did I come
to this desolate place
and give up truth
to gain these walls
that close me in?*

*What price do I pay
to look so strong,
to hide from God?
I cannot pay.
. . . I am empty.*

When my first husband began to withdraw from me emotionally, I was frightened to the core. I began to suspect he was having an affair. However, instead of admitting my fear and confronting his actions, I determined to be a more creative lover, a better housekeeper, a more godly woman. If I could just become the virtuous woman described in Proverbs 31, he'd *have* to stay with me! So I was up every morning at six o'clock having my quiet time, begging God to save my marriage, and listing prayer requests. After fixing biscuits, bacon, and eggs, I packed everybody's lunch and started dinner in the crockpot. Then it was time for the kids' carpool before beginning my full-time job as a school secretary. In between cake decorating and aerobic dance classes, I'd read Christian marriage books. But instead of the anticipated and hoped-for self improvements, I'm afraid I became a "totaled" woman, trying in vain to be a perfect wife.

A year later, after my husband left home, I began to see the convergence of many harmful patterns. Already emotionally divorced from myself, I was on physical and spiritual overload. Rigid attitudes ruthlessly dictated a flawless performance and set me up for failure. And I never quite measured up. Covering up my jealousy and fear with layers of phoniness, I actually thought it was wrong and "unspiritual" to feel these emotions. I didn't know that "in some instances jealousy is more than appropriate; it is the only virtuous reaction to real threats to marriage."[4]

Mechanical Toys and Wind-up People

Once I'd lost at marriage, I wanted to scream at God. It seemed so unfair that I would lose, after trying so hard. *Why did You allow this to happen, God? Why couldn't I have my family together under one roof?*

Why?

I worked so hard at being a good wife and mother, teaching my sons about You, and working in a Christian school, never missing my morning prayer time! Weren't You "watching me?" Didn't I follow the script? Wasn't I a good girl?

One of the methods God uses to interrupt our religious recitations is to allow a crisis into our life's drama. Often, this crisis opens the door to growth and freedom, however painful it feels at the time. Sue Monk Kidd said it so well: "A crisis is an invitation to cross a threshold."[5] A crisis can force us from a starring role in "Let's Pretend" to spontaneously playing a God-directed part in "Being Real."

WWJD

Oftentimes, children give us cues about becoming more Real, more Christlike. When our carefully kept, perfect fur coats of phoniness begin to wear thin in a few spots, we can look to the "little people" for reminders of genuineness. And of all the "little people" in the whole world, Daniel Windsor is one of my very favorites. At six years of age, Daniel has achieved a high level of wisdom, and sometimes my soul has to stand on tiptoe to grasp it. One night while Frank and I were visiting his family, I noticed Daniel's WWJD bracelet, the pop jewelry rage. (The letters stand for "What Would Jesus Do?") "Does this bracelet help you stop and think about what Jesus would do before you get into a fight or say something ugly?" I asked Daniel.

"Naaaw," my young friend replied, with refreshing honesty. "I know I'm *supposed* to say yes. But I'd have to really think about it to stop myself from fighting. This is just for decoration."

Daniel wasn't too eager to give the "right" answer just for the sake of conformity. He's far too genuine for that. His candor reminds me that *God must enjoy my being Real with Him, too.* Besides being a great little buddy to have fun with, Daniel helps me gain courage to lay down my spiritual speech and pour my honest heart out to God.

The Velveteen Woman

Trust is the Opposite of Control

Perhaps you have performed a role with precision, as I did, trying to *earn* love. All the while our Master Director knows that apart from discovering we are deeply loved *without earning or deserving it*, we'll never be fully alive, free to serve and enjoy Him. Unless we stop pursuing a performance of perfection and begin redeeming our "frequent failure coupons" for His forgiveness, we'll never be anything more than a wind-up woman putting on airs, pretending to be Real.

I am so grateful to have received a second chance at marriage—a second opportunity to learn that trust is the opposite of demanding control by following a "religiously correct" script. "In the Bible, God calls people to faith, not certainty," says Don Hudson in a recent article in *Mars Hill Review*. [But] "we all want a father who gives us certainty, though certainty tears us from faith."[6] God wants us to trust in Him. To return to Him over and over in the midst of life's ups and downs. To face up to life as it is, instead of pretending it's how we think it should be. To live intentionally, spontaneously, in the present moment, as His beloved children.

Faith is not the same thing as a denial of reality. Faith has more to do with being fully aware of life as it really is, yet letting go of control and believing God will handle all the areas of my life. It's saying, "I'm scared," when I feel afraid, instead of "I'm fine." One day, this idea of letting go was beautifully illustrated to me by my friend Steve as we ate lunch with some other friends on our back deck. Spring had just blossomed into summer, and the predictable Texas heatwave hadn't yet set in.

"See that pecan tree?" Steve asked. "It's kind of like us. In the fall, all the healthy leaves dropped to the ground, and new growth is now taking their place. The dead branch still has last year's leaves attached," he explained as I peered more closely at the crispy brown leaves still clustered on the branch.

"The dead leaves never got the signal it was time to turn loose."

"You're right," I said after a moment's reflection. "Like those dead, crispy leaves, sometimes we choose to hang onto dead, withering habits instead of letting go and growing into new possibilities." When we release old, worn out ways of doing things, we are free to discover, creatively give our gifts to others, and enjoy the life-giving luxury of intimacy with God.

Mechanical Toys and Wind-up People

Have you ever seen a speaker get up to a podium and read her lines? Or perhaps heard someone recite a memorized speech? Terrified of the audience's disapproval, she concentrates all her effort on one thing: not making mistakes. Perfection has become her top priority.

But do you, like me, ever want to walk up to the stage, pull away the notes, and say, "Would you just relax and talk to us? Just tell us your story. What's on your mind?"

Do you wonder if God sometimes wants to walk up to us, gently pull away our Bible, devotional, or study outline, and say, "Would you just relax and talk to Me? Tell Me your story. What's on your mind?"

I can empathize with both the speaker and the audience. How much simpler it is to read from prepared notes, or recite a canned speech. How uncertain and scary it feels to express, impromptu, straight from my heart. But I'm learning more and more, as I speak before groups, that when I put aside my notes and simply say who I am, where I've come from, what I long for, people are touched. Ministry happens. The Holy Spirit can work through me.

And so, a part of letting go of our perfectionism means we have to relinquish our notes and relax into being ourselves, much the way Steve's tree had to loosen its grip on old dried-up leaves if it wanted to grow fresh ones.

Philip Yancey reminds us that "the opposite of sin is grace—not virtue."[7] And Scott Peck said, "It is not pleasant to be aware of oneself as a naturally lazy, ignorant, self-centered being that rather routinely betrays its Creator, its fellow creatures, and even its own best interests. Yet this unpleasant sense of personal failure and inadequacy is paradoxically the greatest blessing a human being can possess."[8] When I realize I'm a whole lot worse than I ever thought I was, I can finally accept God's love, because it makes grace necessary. Then I can freely open my arms to God's love, instead of trying to earn His approval.

God wants far more from us than a laundry list of good deeds we've performed. He wants our hearts. In *The Sacred Romance*, the authors describe God's deep desire for us this way: "What he is after is us—our laughter, our tears, our dreams, our fears, our heart of hearts. Remember his lament in Isaiah (29:13), that though his people were performing all their duties, 'their hearts are far from me'?"[9] How eagerly God would have exchanged duty for beauty—the beauty of seeing us being Real with Him. He wants us—even with all our rubbed-off patches, bald spots, and shabby sinner's skin. Yes, He wants US—the Real us.

Soaking in our Subject

A few years back, I worked for a short while as secretary to the dean of arts and humanities at a university in Dallas. I learned many valuable life lessons from the late Dean Robert Corrigan. One day, he explained to me how a gifted actress spends many hours researching, rehearsing, and soaking in her subject. Then, when it's time for the performance, the audience no longer sees the performer, but rather the person or thing she represents. It was the difference between an actor trying to impress the audience and learning to express what he or she absorbed.

How well, I wonder, *do we as Christians soak in our subject—the Creator—so that when we play out our unique role in the drama of life, people see Him uniquely reflected in us?*

Even though God is the Mighty Creator of the universe, He's much more gentle than we are. While we often demand, *"Watch Me!"* God lets us choose whether or not we will look to Him for direction. But in His heart of hearts, He longs for us to take our eyes off the script we cling to and receive our moment-to-moment cues from Him, without demanding to know the next lines. That's what trust is. Instead of knowing exactly where our life drama is leading, He wants us to let life unfold scene by scene, line by line. This sort of living exposes little patches of Real skin amongst our fake fur. Tiny windows of Real for others to peek through and see Jesus inside us. And eventually, little by little, to see Jesus uniquely reflected in us.

As for me, I realize I have many more miles to travel before I'm completely Real. But when I come upon roadblocks and rabbit trails, I keep returning to the center of the path. I keep on plodding down the road, one step at a time. Not because I'm strong. Not because I'm good. But because I'm loved.

AS THE BATTLE RAGES 'ROUND ME . . .
I AM GLAD TO HAVE FOUND
THAT I AM NOT THE GENERAL
AND THAT HIS LOVE FOR ME
IS THE SOURCE OF EVERYTHING I NEED.
WITH HIM AS THE GENERAL,
I NEED ONLY LEARN TO SALUTE AND MARCH.
THE CELEBRATION CAN THEN BEGIN—
WHERE THE SALUTE BECOMES THE EMBRACE,
AND THE MARCH BECOMES THE DANCE.[10]

MICHAEL J. KENDALL

Fake Fur Perception:

If I perform well in my starring role of "Let's Pretend," I'll earn God's love and be guaranteed a Happily Ever After ending.

Real Skin Reality:

I become a little more like Jesus as I follow my God-directed part in "Becoming Real" one day at a time.

One evening, while the Rabbit was lying there . . . he saw two strange beings creep out of the tall bracken near him. They were rabbits like himself, but quite furry and brand-new. They must have been very well made, for their seams didn't show at all, and they changed shape in a queer way when they moved . . . instead of always staying the same like he did. The strange rabbit came quite close . . . "He doesn't smell right!" he exclaimed.

CHAPTER 5

Looking Down Our Twitching Noses

Comparisons begin early in life as we measure ourselves against our siblings to see who's the prettiest, the smartest, the most popular. As we enter the worlds of school and work, the competition intensifies. Who got the best report card, the latest job promotion, the handsomest boyfriend become critically important. Like the Velveteen Rabbit peeking out of the bracken to see the strange, furry, brand-new looking bunnies, we happen upon others who are different from us. Noting that their seams don't show at all, and marveling at their abilities, we look at our own stuff and fluff (and seams and flaws) and sink with the comparison.

I've heard it said, "Almost all of our unhappiness is the result of comparing ourselves to others." When we play the comparison game, we see ourselves as either *better than* or *worse than* the other person. Whether we end up on top or on bottom, it's a lose-lose deal. Instead of just being our "real skin" selves, we may try being superior, "one upping" others by declaring that we have the inside track on truth and spirituality. Or, we may settle into feelings of inferiority, habitually "one-downing" ourselves—spending our days trying to force our own unique little rabbit feet into the footprints of others. If you aren't quite sure how to find your unique path to Real, how to identify your inner passions right now, it's okay. We'll explore these ideas further in a later chapter. For now, see if you can identify in yourself, as I do in myself, some ways you fall into comparisons.

Feeling Inferior

I once thought the spiritual life was beyond the harmful blows of comparison. The workings of the soul seemed somehow out of reach of mindless haggling over who's good, better, or best. Oh, if only this were true. Actually, I think we're especially vulnerable to comparisons of each other's inner life, since there's really no way to measure, evaluate, or assign a grade to "soul growth."

But God is not interested in formulas and measurements. He just wants us to find satisfaction in His love and acceptance, and to respond to Him out of *gratitude*. Until we catch onto this simple but profound truth, we'll continue looking around, sniffing and whiffing at others to see how we measure up.

Bonnie's face glowed as she spoke. I was sitting in the large audience at the women's retreat, listening to her speak passionately about her pursuit of intimacy with God.

"I've never experienced such joy," she said, radiantly.

"For me, the key to finding closeness to God is to spend more time in contemplative prayer."

After the retreat, I asked my friend Sarah to take a walk along the shore of the lake. For a while we walked in silence, then Sarah stopped, folded her arms, and stared, as her eyes fixed on some faraway place.

"How come nothing happens to me when I try to spend a long time in prayer? Why don't I have Bonnie's joy? Why don't I glow like she does?"

"You seem to feel less spiritual than Bonnie because your experience is different," I commented, remembering many times when I also one-downed myself. Sarah's trancelike state left me wondering if she could even hear my words. "Remember, you're at a different life stage than she is," I went on. "With two toddlers running around, it may not be easy to make time for things like contemplative prayer.

Sarah admired Bonnie's seemingly sleek spirit. As she compared her own relationship with God to Bonnie's, Sarah felt inferior, as if all her velveteen seams were coming apart at the contrast. A few weeks passed before I talked with Sarah again. When we met for a mid-afternoon snack, it didn't take me long to notice that her countenance had taken on a glow of its own.

"I think I'm beginning to see some moments of joy in my own life, through the eyes of my children," Sarah explained, unaware of her radiance. Sarah went on to say that her three-year-old adopted daughter had recently been playing with her favorite doll, wrapping her up in a cozy blanket and tucking her into bed. Suddenly, she'd stopped her play and glanced up to see Sarah looking on. Then, she'd happily declared, "I'm so glad to have you for my mommy!" pointing proudly to her adoptive mom.

Looking Down Our Twitching Noses

"I suppose I've just ignored my children's enthusiasm for life," my friend said, pausing to gather her thoughts about the two little ones she and her husband had adopted just six months earlier. "But you know, they give me little reflections of God's love in sweet, everyday ways. I guess I was looking for a more serious spiritual experience, like what some other women describe, instead of noticing what God was placing right before my eyes." Sarah went on, "This time, I got down on my three year old's eye level and told her, 'I'm so happy to have you too!'" As this young mom began to let go of comparisons, she freed herself to discover little windows of God's joy in the middle (and muddle!) of mothering.

Do you ever catch yourself looking for a "serious spiritual experience?" One that looks better than your own? I've heard lots of frustrated young moms make comments similar to Sarah's, and later rejoice as they found satisfaction in accepting their current stage in life. Mothers of preschoolers don't often have a lot time for contemplating, so if you're in this stage of life, don't compare yourself to a woman at midlife or beyond who has more free time and more choices. Notice how Sarah found "reflections of God's love" right there in her own home, once she gave up the comparison game. Right there in her child's face, before her very eyes. She just needed to slow down and look for Jesus in her life.

The Need to Feel Superior

THE GREATER A PERSON'S SENSE OF GUILT, THE GREATER HIS NEED
TO CAST BLAME ON OTHERS.

ANONYMOUS

Martha and her husband dropped by for a visit on a lazy Sunday afternoon. Before long, our conversation settled on the subject of spiritual life.

"You need to seek a certain spiritual gift (she named one) if you want intimacy with God," Martha flatly declared. Like one of the furry, brand-new bunnies approaching the Velveteen Rabbit in the story, Martha came up to us, took one whiff, and exclaimed, "You don't smell right! You need to do it like I'm doing it! This is the only right way!"

As Frank and I looked curiously at each other, I was sure we shared the same thought: *What's so wrong with my spiritual life?* "Tell us about your experience," I reluctantly coaxed, like a timid child acting brave, but filled with self-doubt. I struggled to listen and affirm my friend, without "one-downing" myself. It wasn't easy.

As we search for closeness with God, we won't all find it in the same way. Author and pastor Steve Brown said, "It is important that you recognize that one can't live the Christian life without prayer. But don't let anybody, except God, define for you what your prayer life ought to be."[1] In rabbit words, don't let anyone look down their twitching nose at you! God is the only one who has a right to do this, and He chose not to.

In a public address, Henri Nouwen once said, "In a football game, if you are the winner, the other guy is the loser. But that's not true with God."[2] Each of us is a winning recipient of His unconditional love. What is your motivation for "winning?" For teaching Sunday School? For speaking at the women's retreat? For volunteering to be president of the P.T.A.? Are you striving to be best, or to be Real?

Perhaps the trademark of true inner passion is a focus on God's love, instead of on winning. This outlook naturally edges out a critical, judgmental spirit. Like water bubbling up from a natural spring, we feel at home in our own spiritual skin when we respond to God from our hearts. To God, we are all beloved. With or without trophies. Finely finished or frayed at the velveteen seams.

A Report Card for Sinners

"Sometimes the place where I feel the least myself is at church," a vulnerable pastor once said. In the church, we often assign some sort of grading system to sins. It's as if we view God as a giant Professor saying, "Okay, you were divorced, so you get a D. Sit in the back row! If all you did was gossip, then you get a B. Sit in the second row! And if you happen to be struggling with homosexuality, you flunk. You'll have to sit outside in the hallway!"

For me, there have been times when I held this view of God. When I made myself feel better by comparing my "sin report card" to others who were failing more conspicuously than I.

"Hello, Brenda? This is Paul. Can we talk?"

"Sure, come on over to my office," I spoke into the receiver. "I'll have some free time this afternoon."

Hanging up the phone, I tried to remember the last time I'd seen Paul. He'd taught my sons junior high math at the Christian school. He'd been a good friend and confidante. I'd heard rumors that he was gay, and now my thoughts were jumbled. *Why does he want to talk to me? What will I say if . . .*

"Hey, Bren-da-da!" Paul gave me his usual warm greeting.

"Paul, it's so good to see you." I moved forward to give him a hug, then got quickly to the point. "I've heard rumors. What's going on?" I asked.

"Brenda," Paul sighed as he gathered his thoughts. He looked exhausted. "I've been through hell. You have no idea, and I won't give you the details now. You know I'm a Christian, right?"

"Sure, Paul, I know you're a Christian," I affirmed, recalling days when we'd discussed our mutual faith in Christ. Paul shifted uncomfortably in his chair.

"Well, to tell you the truth, I'm confused. I have lots of questions," Paul cried out. "And the thing is—they won't let me in the church. I'm trying to find answers!" He paused for a moment, then lowered his voice and added thoughtfully, "Look. I admit I don't *know* that I'm right. I may be wrong. Like I said, I'm confused."

"Paul, you're living in sin," I hastened to assert. "You *are* wrong. It says so in the Bible." I could see Paul's disappointment in my response. He quickly switched the conversation to surface issues and after a few minutes of small talk, Paul said he had to go.

I didn't see Paul for a couple of years after that conversation. Later, I heard that he'd been offended by my comments. In a moment of reflection, I recalled the discrimination I had once felt when I went through divorce. While close friends showered me with a single parent's delights—free car repairs, Christmas money for the kids, baby-sitting, and dinner invitations—there were those who looked on with less tolerance. In some circles, the "D word" was the unpardonable sin—the kind that could get you kicked out of the holy classroom. I wondered if, in my visit with Paul that day, I'd taken my chance to "one-up" a brother, at his emotional expense.

Recalling how Jesus related to outcasts of His time, and the tender lovingkindness God had shown to me during my divorce, I felt more compassionate toward Paul. A couple of years passed. I didn't see Paul or talk with him. Then a mutual friend died, and Paul and I both attended the funeral. Afterward, I asked if we could talk. He agreed, reluctantly. Grateful for a chance to clarify my friendship with Paul, I brushed off a clean spot on the concrete church steps, and we both sat down.

"Tell me how I offended you," I coaxed.

"You condemned me," Paul said, his eyes fixed on mine. "I would not have expected you to approve of my lifestyle, so *that* wasn't the problem. But you condemned *me* as a person!" Tears welled up in Paul's eyes.

"I'm sorry," I confessed, letting my own tears fall freely. "I care about you, Paul. Forgive me?"

"It wasn't like you to just write me off like that!" he said, dodging my apology. "I tried to understand why you'd be so harsh, but I couldn't. I didn't expect you to approve of my *actions,* but I thought I could count on your friendship," he concluded.

"I'm so sorry, Paul," I repeated sincerely, recoiling internally as I remembered how Jesus hated sin. But oh, how He loved all of us sinners.

After a long pause, Paul began to nod slowly. "Okay," he said, reaching to embrace me. "Hey, friend. Yeah. I forgive you."

It took a few moments for us to regain composure. "I know you are looking for answers, and I trust you will find them," I said, smiling through my tears.

As I left Paul that day, I took with me a warm feeling of acceptance I hadn't come with. We were both on the same level, both sinners in need of God's grace. Neither of us was superior, nor inferior. We were just brother and sister.

In our Sunday School class one day shortly after my reunion with Paul, the subject of homosexuality came up. A certain man in the group arrogantly declared, "I think we should just line 'em all up and shoot 'em!"

A few people added a hearty "Amen!" and the subject was closed. A few weeks later, we were on a weekend trip with a couple from the Sunday School class. The topic of homosexuality came up again.

"I think the guy in our class who said we should just line 'em up and shoot 'em was right on!" our friend stated emphatically.

"Oh really?" I asked, curious, wondering if he was struggling himself, though perhaps not about his sexuality. About being one-up. "What if they are people looking for answers?" I pressed him. "How about if they're really searching for truth?" I'd learned my lesson painfully. For me, homosexuality now had *real skin* on, and a familiar face. "The issue, for me, is not whether homosexuality is wrong or right. I know what the Scriptures say. But how will we relate to people who are wrestling with homosexuality? What would Jesus do?"

The next week, our travel companion brought me a three-page list of Scripture verses condemning the practice of homosexuality. If we'd discussed the same topic a couple of years earlier, I'd probably have thoughtlessly agreed, "Yep, look at all those verses that prove how bad those people are." But now Paul—a friend—was one of the condemned people in the line-up, waiting to be assassinated for the sin of struggling.

"Homosexuality is clearly wrong," I agreed with our friend, "just as adultery and gossip are wrong. So, how will we as Christians relate to people who are struggling in this way?"

This time, my friend had no answer.

Values, Standards, and Pigeon Poop

"We've got to have standards in the church!" I've often heard, and it's so true. But standards are about behavior and attitudes, not *the value of people*. "Hate the sin, love the sinner" is often spouted but seldom fleshed out in the body of Christ. We want to feel superior, so we find

63

someone else to condemn. Someone who is divorced, or struggling with homosexuality or some other sin we've not yet encountered.

Instead of simply believing we are really precious to God, we may get sidetracked, clinging to our need to compare. Trying to show God what good girls and boys we are, especially next to the really bad kids in the world's classroom.

Jesus used no such grading system for sins. He said we're all in need of His blood for cleansing. Instead of arrogantly one-upping others, Jesus shared intimate moments of table fellowship with sinners. "By accepting them as friends and equals, Jesus (took) away their shame, humiliation, and guilt."[3] And when He spoke about comparisons, Jesus said we should be very careful, because it's easy to see a smudge on our neighbor's face while we are oblivious to the sneers and smears on our own.[4] He said we shouldn't throw rocks at another person, unless we can say we are free and clear of all sin.[5] The truth is, we're all just shabby sinners.

Still, we continue checking each other over for smudges, and picking up rocks to throw. And amazingly, God keeps on loving us just the same.

———

During a counseling session, Stan brought up the issue of his need to compare himself to others. He told this story:

"I was at the gas station, in a hurry to get to the airport and catch a plane. I'd just pumped some gas and went into the lobby to pay. Three other people were ahead of me. One was having difficulty deciding which brand of cigarettes to buy, another was buying lotto tickets and taking the time to rub them off at the counter, and one man was just waiting patiently to pay for his gas.

"I thought, *Here we go again,* anxiously checking my watch. *If God would just take care of these sinners, the world would be a much better place! If it weren't for the lottery and cigarettes, I'd be on my way.* After a few minutes of waiting, I paid for the gas and stormed out the lobby door, still mumbling to God, *Why don't you DO SOMETHING about these sinners!* I got in my car, slammed the transmission into gear, and screeched off.

"As I did, I heard a loud noise. *FOOP!* I glanced in my rearview mirror and saw that the gas hose had clanged to the ground after I made my quick getaway, with the nozzle still stuck in my tank. At that same moment, I felt something wet on the back of my neck. Reaching my hand back to touch the wet place, I felt a large glob of pigeon poop which was apparently deposited while I filled my tank."

With a big smile, Stan summed up the humorous tale this way: "God put me in my place. He reminded me that I'm no better than anybody else. I'm just one of those sinners. Some of us are hung up on cigarettes and the lottery, while others are judgmental Pharisees who get their nozzles hung up at the gas tank. So God occasionally sends a pigeon along to remind us we're all on the same level—in need of His grace."

The facade of superiority is just as ugly to God (and maybe more so) than the visible sins we like to condemn. Could it be that God is more grieved when His church patronizes pride and favoritism than He is by all the smoking, drinking, and gambling that goes on in the whole world? Could it be that He is not at all impressed by our sneers of superiority? "Dying to self" means crucifying this facade. Learning to recognize ways we deny our vulnerability so we can feel superior.

When we "size up" other people, looking down our twitching noses at them, we're really just exposing our own smallness. Our critical comments only advertise our weakness and insecurity. Nothing silences the judgmental voice of comparisons like God's unconditional acceptance. The more we soak in His love, the easier it is to respond to Him naturally, freely, passionately. Regardless of how hard we try, we are never good enough to be worthy of God's love. But He is worthy. He is enough.

And now, let's take a closer look at one type of comparison most women struggle with, for "appearances" sake. . . .

THANK YOU, LORD, FOR NOT JUDGING ME
BY MY FAKE FUR AND SHABBY SELF-RIGHTEOUSNESS.
THANK YOU FOR LOVING THE REAL SKIN ME.

Fake Fur
Perception:

I may be inferior to some people, but as long as
I'm superior to most, God will love me.

Real Skin
Reality:

When I compare myself to others, I always lose.
To God, I am precious. What can compare
with that kind of acceptance?

There was once a
Velveteen Rabbit, and in the
beginning he was really splendid . . .
On Christmas morning, when
the Rabbit sat wedged in the
top of the Boy's stocking,
with a sprig of holly between
his paws, the effect was charming.

CHAPTER 6

Spiritual Cosmetics

One of my favorite literary classics is *Anne of Green Gables.* I suppose I can identify with Anne Shirley's strong-willed determination and stubbornness, as well as her vivid imagination and love of timeless prose. Perhaps you can identify with Anne, as well. Like most of us, she would have liked to change a thing or two about her appearance. Especially her red hair, which Anne believed God gave to her "on purpose."

"Hey, Carrots!" a classmate named Gilbert Blythe teased on Anne's first day at her new school.

In a desperate attempt to rid herself of the "curse" once and for all, Anne bought a bottle of hair dye from the local peddler who promised it would turn her red hair raven black, like Diana's, her closest friend. When the dye turned Anne's hair *green* instead, she sank to the depths of despair. Now, she was really desperate! Green hair was even worse than red! Alas, it was time for a haircut . . .

Near the end of the book, Gilbert Blythe again called Anne "Carrots." But this time it was in the context of a loving overture. They had grown up, and Anne had developed an appreciation for her internal qualities: a love of good books, courage, and an active mind. The more-grown-up Anne simply smiled at the comment, and took the smitten young man's hand in her own.

The shift from an external to an internal focus takes more years of living for most of us than it did for Anne Shirley. At sixteen, the brave girl with a pioneering spirit had done as much self-exploration as I would do in more than four decades.

"Who's the prettiest?" the second grade girls asked, as they formed a circle of grinning faces around their teacher. Miss Shanks smiled affectionately.

"You're all pretty to me. Now, let's not have a contest!"

But off we ran, giggling, eagerly seeking our next target to encircle. I was the chubby one (cube-shaped, actually) with the Buster Brown haircut. I still occasionally recall the pain that stabbed my tender little girl's heart the day Linda Langston announced to me, "You can't play! Go away, Fatty!" Ouch. Childhood nicknames can leave stinging memories.

You probably have a similar childhood story—the kind that still leaves you wincing a bit, even after decades have passed. Maybe you had big lips, so you decided to sort of curl them in as you talked, hoping nobody would notice them. Or maybe your hair was a color you hated, as was the case with Anne Shirley. Or too curly, so you spent hours ironing it or rolling it up on orange juice cans to make it straighter. Although I managed to shed some of my early childhood pudginess, by junior high I'd gone to the *other* extreme, shooting up taller than all the boys. "Giraffe," became my new nickname.

At sixteen, an age when Anne Shirley spent hours reading Tennyson on the grounds of Green Gables, my goal in life was to become the high school homecoming queen. Leaving my rhinestone-rimmed glasses at home, I'd squint at the blackboard from the front row, preferring to strain my eyes rather than give up my goal of being a beauty queen. My short swim-and-go hairstyle grew into the popular backcombed bubble bouffant. In the school hallways, I'd smile broadly, showing all my recently straightened teeth, both to those I liked and those I didn't. The true focus of my efforts: to be pretty and popular.

I had a lot to learn about real beauty.

I wish I could say things have changed a lot in thirty years, that I've completely shed the quest for good looks. (Sometimes becoming a cheerleader or homecoming queen can magnify the importance of good looks, and make it harder to let go of our culture's fake fur notions of what it means to be a lovely woman.) For years, I imagined my sparkling queen's crown and short rah-rah skirt would still fit, and that I could run through those pompom routines without gasping for breath.

By the time I reached the fourth decade of my life, the truth hit hard. I would grow old. Though my looks were never anything to rave about, I had come to count on my appearance as a way of earning acceptance.

Oh, if only Miss Shanks' words could be taken seriously, and we women would quit making a contest of our looks. But most of us make at least some kind of effort to look like the fashion models we see extolled on the covers of magazines. Trouble is, fashion changes from day to day, decade to decade. Curly hair becomes more popular than straight. Like the fat and bunchy Velveteen Rabbit on Christmas morning, the chubby models of the Victorian era once expressed the cultural view of a "charming effect." After a time, the Twiggy look became the desirable image. Like the revolving glass door in your favorite department store, the "in look" keeps changing, going around, coming around, and going around again.

In Louisa May Alcott's classic story *Little Women*, the wise Mrs. March voices to her daughters Meg, Jo, and Amy, a timeless culture-free definition of beauty which women—of any era—are longing to hear from their mothers:

I only care what you think of yourself. If you feel your value lies in being merely decorative, I fear that someday you might find yourself believing that's all that you really are. Time erodes all such beauty. But what it cannot diminish is the wonderful workings of your mind—your humor, your kindness, and your moral courage. These are the things I cherish so in you.

Unfortunately, many of our moms never even claimed these inner truths for themselves, let alone understood the importance of passing them on to their daughters. So we continued to listen to our culture's definition of beauty, unwittingly paying a far higher price than the cost of bottles and jars of cosmetics.

Many years after I left Miss Shanks' class, the phantom creature who began stalking me on the elementary school playground was still around. *You must lose weight,* she hissed. *You must look good.* Battling this predator would be far more complicated than telling myself looks weren't all that important. Many women and adolescent girls today are fighting the same war.

Pretty Woman

Marissa, a sixteen-year-old beauty sat nervously in my office.

She'd come in for treatment of an eating disorder. With facial features that resembled Cindy Crawford and the body to match, it was hard to imagine she felt so out of control. Marissa fit today's perfect model description: tall, thin, flawless complexion, "big hair," full lips, large breasts.

The Velveteen Woman

"I don't know why I have to talk to you!" Marissa glared at me. "I don't need any help! My mom is just on my case because I throw up once in a while."

It would be weeks before Marissa trusted me enough to begin to open up. To confess how dirty and flawed she felt if her appearance wasn't absolutely perfect.

With halting sobs, she finally cried out in desperation, "Please help me!" The fear-stricken girl began to unload, bit by bit. Marissa wept about the overwhelming sense of shame and guilt that consumed her each time she performed her "cleansing ritual," in which she would tie her hair back, and line up seven glasses full of water on the bathroom vanity. The water would make her feel full, and help her purge more easily. Marissa had learned that beauty was one way to earn her alcoholic father's approval. *If I can just be pretty enough, maybe daddy will stop drinking,* she reasoned to herself. But as time passed, she had to admit that her plan wasn't working.

Women with eating disorders have typically endured a shameful past. Perhaps you don't suffer in this way, but were wounded by some other kind of hurtful girlhood experience. One day over lunch, a woman shared with me that she gained weight during her junior high years, (oh, those wonderfully traumatic, hormone-injected junior high years!) so her dad bribed her: he'd give her a dollar for every pound she lost. Another friend said her overweight mom pressured her to be sexy and gorgeous. When this young woman refused to get breast implants at age twenty-one, her mother was furious.

These kinds of experiences can hurt deeply. In reaction to pain, some of us have declared that beauty does not matter, or even gone so far as to announce that beauty is evil. But no matter how we struggle, physical beauty continues to matter. Even to those who appear to have it in the most generous portions. "Marilyn Monroe went to nightclubs disguised in a black wig long after she was famous to see if she could still attract a man as Norma Jean. She felt the emptiness as soon as she was no longer being flirted with, even after clearly establishing her identity as the world's most beautiful woman. And the emptiness consumed her in the end."[1] It's not *wrong* to try to look pretty. But if we're really trying to fill a gaping emotional vacuum that can only be filled with love, we'll find our efforts to be beautiful just another roadblock to becoming Real.

———

Carol was a beautiful twenty-five-year-old woman with a voluptuous body. As we worked together in the same office, I often noticed how she lit up when men noticed her, but then wilted again when she wasn't getting attention. One morning she came to the office crying. "My boyfriend broke up with me." Though I listened to Carol and tried to encourage her, she didn't seem to hear a thing I said. It was as if she were playing an old, out-of-date tape in her mind over and over as she lamented, "I'm fat. I'm ugly. That's why he doesn't love me anymore."

If the truth be known, it is often the pretty woman who's driven by an enormous lack of inner security, a compulsion to use facial make-up as a skilled artist, or an addiction to relentless exercise to keep her body looking great. If a woman thinks her looks are all she has, she will focus all her efforts on making the most of them. Like young Anne Shirley, the pretty woman has succumbed to the advertising peddler, buying bottles of faddish "sure cure" for her beauty dilemmas. Only problem is, she never gets the results she really wants. There's still that lingering, gnawing sense of self-doubt inside. Sort of like green hair dye that won't wash out.

The Other Side of Evil

Though beauty can pose danger to both women and men, we cannot say that God never uses physical beauty to bring glory to Himself. As a reminder that He will not be stereotyped, figured out, or put into a box, the Bible includes the story of Esther, a young Jewish girl who won both a beauty contest and God's favor, becoming a queen. And the Song of Solomon depicts a lover's wild and uninhibited celebration of his bride's body, which was gorgeous, at least to him.

In the beginning, we were created to be beautiful, naked, shameless. As daughters of Eve, our inborn longing for beauty is a natural part of ourselves, dating back to the Garden of Eden. In *Perelandra*, C.S. Lewis' sophisticated fantasy that deals with the age-old problem of temptation, the beauty of Eve is described this way:

There was no category in the terrestrial mind which would fit her. Opposites met in her and were fused in a fashion for which we have no images. One way of putting it would be to say that neither our sacred nor our profane art could make her portrait. Beautiful, naked, shameless, young—she was obviously a goddess: but then the face, the face so calm that it escaped insipidity by the very concentration of its mildness, the face that was like the sudden coldness and stillness of a church when we enter it from a hot street—that made her a Madonna. The alert, inner silence which looked out from those eyes overawed him; yet at any moment she might laugh like a child, or run like Artemis or dance like a Maenad.[2]

The Velveteen Woman

Physical beauty was originally intended to be our birthright as daughters of Eve. It's natural to long for physical beauty. But in a fallen world, the longing too often turns to a consuming jealousy, enslaving both women and men. Beauty—a gift from the Creator—was spoiled by sin.

Am I Lovely? Do You Want Me?

From the time we were separated from God—our First Love—we have been plagued by gnawing questions that reflect our self-doubt. The authors of *The Sacred Romance* aptly describe this sense of a woman's self-questioning: *Am I lovely? Do you want me?*[3] If a woman has been divorced, or rejected by an overly strict or emotionally absent father, she may have received the painful message, "No. You are not lovely. I don't want you." Some women spend many years searching for a "yes" response, exploiting femininity.

In the popular movie *First Wives Club*, there is a sad, yet funny contemporary illustration of women trying hard not to need the men who rejected them. Each of the three women in the club has a different strategy for making her life work better without her ex-husband. Elise spent a lot of time and money being beautiful and got her share of strokes for it.

"Elise! You look SO GOOD!" were words she loved to hear. Following in Cher's footsteps, Elise had been yanked, stitched, stuffed, and pulled to make herself look younger and better. She'd had every kind of lift and implant invented, including gargantuan collagen injections to make her lips look fuller, so full, in fact, they rather took over the bottom half of her delicate face!

The movie ends as the three women declare their independence and assert their strength to rise above rejection from their husbands: "You Don't Own Me," they sing out in three-part harmony.

Before clucking our critical tongues and pointing an accusing finger at these three women's libbers, stop a moment and think how often we relate to God *just like this.* Unsure that He really loves us unconditionally, we keep a coping strategy handy. *How can we make our life work without Him,* we wonder, *just in case He lets us down?*

Some of us have come to think of God as we think of men we've known and loved, and been let down by. Then, like the disappointed trio in *First Wives Club,* we're fearful of needing Him. Afraid that we'll be set aside, like the Velveteen Rabbit, when better looking "toys" came along.

Perhaps you have experienced more than your fair share of rejection from men. The notion of a reckless love without any limits seems beyond belief—like a fairy tale. Just as the young Anne Shirley didn't care much for God because He gave her red hair "on purpose," you may be holding God at arm's length because deep down inside you feel rejected. Others have abandoned you in the past, and God let it all happen. It can seem like He did so "on purpose."

But we needn't be so suspicious. God is the only one who will never, ever leave us, no matter what. We are His beloved. To Him, we are always beautiful.

The Call of our First Love

Our deepest need is to know we are loved. Funny, how the simple truths can take a lifetime to soak in. But that seems to be the deal. The process of appreciating our inner beauty develops gradually, bit by bit. After my faith crisis, when I began to get the message that Jesus loves me, my desire for inner beauty became greater than any desire I may have had for a face lift. I began to understand that I can't impress God with make-up or nail polish or Bible memory verses. That there are no spiritual cosmetics. Unselfconscious grace, an inner focus, enjoying a unique personal style—these are the ageless beauty marks God appreciates in us.

A woman's true beauty is her feminine response to the call of her First Love. "Others may leave you, but I will never reject you or leave you," God says. "I love you. Not because you look so good, or because you do so many good things, or because you're so successful. I love you, because I love you, because I love you, because I love you."[4]

The
Velveteen
Woman

This is the voice we listen for. This voice must be allowed to grow stronger than all the voices of culture hissing *You must be thin. You must be pretty.* The call of our First Love, that gentle, beckoning whisper, must somehow be heard over the media hype and advertising peddlers who try to convince us that beauty comes in a jar.

"You are my beloved," He says.

"Yes, I want you.

"Oh yes, you are desirable."

Father Hunger

I often recommend a book called *Father Hunger* to clients who struggle with body image, and to the people who care about them. The book addresses the emptiness women sometimes experience when their fathers were emotionally absent, and how this phenomenon can lead to unrealistic ideas about size and weight. It encourages emotional honesty between daughters and their fathers.[5] If you are struggling with a relationship, past or present, with your father, you may be stuck with unresolved issues about beauty and a false view of God as your Father.

God is not here with skin on. But we can grow into an intimate experiential relationship with Him as our Father. The kind of Father who listens and hears. Who understands and cares deeply. Who wants to connect with us in a way that causes us to feel loved by Him.

Are you walking around with a growing hunger inside? It is *His* voice you are hungry to hear. "God's love . . . enables us to accept ourselves the way He's made us and to appreciate the goodness of His image made real in us for eternity."[6] In this fallen world, we need to come to Him often, several times a day, to quell our self-doubts about our worth and our femininity.

As time passes, I realize I will grow old, and very shabby. I may have a past that's checkered with failure and mistakes, and a body checkered with patches of cellulite, wrinkles, and age spots. But all of that will be okay, as long as I can hear the voice of my First Love, who calls me His beloved.

LET THE BEAUTY OF THE LORD OUR GOD BE UPON US.

PSALM 90:17 (NKJV)

Fake Fur Perception:

A godly woman knows that beauty is vain and undesirable.
It is evil to pursue physical beauty.

Real Skin Reality:

While women have an inborn longing to be desirable and
beautiful, physical beauty fades. The shift from an external to an
internal focus may take many years for a woman, but God looks on
the heart. To Him, the Real US creates the most charming effect.

There was a person called Nana, who ruled the nursery. Sometimes she took no notice of the playthings lying about, and sometimes, she went swooping about like a great wind and hustled them away in cupboards. She called this tidying up, and the playthings all hated it.

CHAPTER 7

Nana Tidies Up

What's the first image that pops into your mind when you hear the word, "Nana?" A sweet older lady with a wrinkled face and twinkling eyes, who loves to bake cookies and read stories to children? Me, too. Unfortunately, the Nana in *The Velveteen Rabbit* was far from the Nana of my imagination. Swooping through the nursery, hurriedly tossing the toys into cupboards to clean up, Nana ruled the place.

In this chapter, we'll consider the "Nanas" who often subtly swoop through our lives to tidy us up, tell us who we are, and pressure us to be who we are not. Nana can be an overbearing boss who will not respect limits you set on your work hours. Or a brother or sister in Christ who is eager to "fix" you, and can't accept the untidiness of your life. Or even a manipulative spouse. Like a great gusty wind, Nana swoops about, hustling the Real you away into a cupboard. And, if you're like me (or if you're like all the playthings in the nursery with the Velveteen Rabbit), you really hate it.

Aurora Greenway was a gutsy, gusty, Nana-type in her role in *The Evening Star*. After her daughter's death, Aurora took up the slack raising her grandchildren. For all her controlling and meddling in each of their lives, Aurora gave them mixed signals: *I love you; I reject you. You're capable; you can't handle life without my help.* It drove the kids crazy.

"You can love 'em, but you can't live their lives," warned Rosie, the housekeeper and longtime family friend, when Aurora's grand-daughter, Mellie, protested her constant manipulation.

"Neither can they," responded Aurora, flatly. In her direct but non-intrusive way, Rosie told Aurora that her grandkids hated her meddling, cover-ups, and endless quick fixes. But Aurora was unwilling to hear Rosie's wise words. She wanted neat, tidy, perfect grandchildren. When one of them ended up in prison and another attempted suicide, the clutter of life could no longer be swooped away into the closet.

Some Nanas aren't as easy to recognize as Aurora Greenway. But it's important that we know who they are. Not so we can blame them for all our faults, but so we can pull ourselves free from the bondage of pleasing Nana. As long as we are busy living the not-really-me-but-tidy life, we never get around to becoming Real.

The Tidied-up Me

I DID NOT LOSE MYSELF ALL AT ONCE. I RUBBED OUT MY FACE OVER THE YEARS WASHING AWAY MY PAIN, THE SAME WAY CARVINGS ON STONE ARE WORN DOWN BY WATER[1].

AMY TAN

Ken brought his wife, Sally, in for individual therapy. "My wife needs counseling," he stated, on their initial visit. "I'll just be waiting out here (he pointed toward the waiting room) until you're done."

Like a sick puppy being dropped off at the vet, Sally entered my office and seated herself on the couch, large, sad eyes reflecting a defeated spirit. She'd been dragged to a counselor's office to be fixed. Ironically, successful therapy is really more like unfixing. Unraveling the choking tentacles of chaos, confusion, and unauthenticity that have wrapped themselves around a life.

"How can I help you?" I asked.

"Well, I can't seem to do anything right. I can't even get my work done at home," Sally replied in a soft, monotone voice.

"Tell me more. What kind of work are you trying to accomplish?" I probed.

"Ken gives me a list of chores to get done every day and when he comes home, even though I've had all day, I never seem to get them done. I don't know what's wrong with me."

Apparently, Sally had taken the role of homemaker. Although a traditional model works well in many marriages, it can create boredom or stifle a person's spirit if their heart is not in it.

"What do you think the problem is?" I questioned.

"I'm not sure. I know it's my fault, but I just can't get things done!" she replied, her frustration mounting.

After a few weeks, I asked Ken to join Sally in their counseling sessions. Although he wanted her to be a housewife, as it turned out, Sally wanted a job outside the home. When her husband would not discuss the matter, Sally responded by withdrawing, procrastinating, and self-blaming. Ken had good intentions, but in reality, he was a "Nana" determined to tidy up his wife. He was out to fix her (or in this case, get me to fix her) so she'd be his idea of a good little housewife. Not only was Sally stifling her own personality, she had lost the courage to protest.

Instead of offering our Real selves to others, many of us become like Sally. We offer a tidied up ME, covered with masks, or layers of phoniness. It doesn't seem enough to just be *in process*. We desire a finished product, even if it's not genuine. But inside, we hate it. Living inauthentically is miserable.

Why, then, do so many of us get caught in a Nana's swoop? Why are we so afraid of just relaxing and being ourselves? Often the most powerful question in a woman's therapy, one that usually takes a while to get to, and one that marks a turning point in her healing is this: *What blocks you from believing you are a lovable person?* The answers are always a little different, depending on the person's unique life experience. But at their core, the responses are remarkably similar. In a little book called *Why Am I Afraid To Love?*, John Powell reflects our internal fear of being ourselves with these poignant words: "*If I show you the real me, what if you reject me? It's all I have.*"[2]

My Real self is all I have. So it can be scary to let you have a peek at the Real me. A Nana's hustling and bustling can appear much safer, even if it results in *extreme* behaviors—a telltale sign that a person is living in fear. By their extreme efforts at image keeping, fearful people actually reflect a lack of balance and absence of inner peace. Extremely neat people or extremely sloppy ones; overly controlling people (running others' lives), or those being exceptionally passive (letting others run their lives), are not living authentically, reflecting their genuine selves.

As you look at your own life, does the following statement ring true for you? "God can use me just as I am today. Not when I get tidied up, when I finish my Ph.D., when I get my kids through college, or

when I become a good mother. But just as I am today!" Or are you caught up in a Nana's swoop, living life out of balance? Have you ever wondered how God might feel when we let others tidy us up, fix us according to *their* plan? After all, He is our Maker, our Lover, and our Friend. Should we not ask Him about His plan for us before listening to others who try to tell us who we must be?

If you are under a Nana's control, here's some encouragement. She may come bustling into your life with her quick fixes, but at any moment you can *choose* to get out of her way—to step out of her line of fire. She can do all the swooping she wants, but if you remove yourself from her path, she won't affect you. In other words, it's OUR responsibility to claim the right to be the women God created us to be. It can be difficult. But no price is too high to pay for the privilege of being ourselves.

As Sally and Ken each focused their energy on discovering their God-given uniquenesses, their lives became less chaotic and their self-esteem increased. A while after they'd discontinued therapy, Sally phoned to say she was performing in a community playhouse production. She was on her way to discovering, gradually, the joy of living under God's direction instead of Nana's manipulation.

In Need of Restoration

In his work restoring old hot rods and classic cars, my husband occasionally has the opportunity to influence young men, one at a time. Frank hires a high school student as a helper, but over the course of months and years, the boy gains more than a skill. A strong bond is established between the apprentice and his master craftsman. It's a guy thing. One such young man is a boy I'll call Tommy.

Frank had known Tommy since he was quite young. During his high school years he came to work with Frank to earn some spending money. He lived with his mom and stepbrother. After two marriages, his mom resigned herself to the life of a single parent. Although Tommy was a hard worker at fourteen (when he began working with Frank), he seemed to lose his motivation when he hit about sixteen. Tommy's dad lived in another town, so the distance didn't allow them much time together. The lack of a male role model became increasingly evident as

Tommy approached high school graduation. He had no ambition. No plans. No dreams.

When Tommy graduated, he quit working for Frank. By this time, Frank had developed a deep affection for the young man and was sorry to see him go. Although Tommy promised to visit, years passed, and we didn't see much of him. Through our small town grapevine, we heard that Tommy had not gone to college, wasn't working a regular job, and still lived at home with his mom.

One Sunday afternoon in early October, we heard a car pulling up into our gravel driveway. It sounded like an old pick-up with a loud, rumbling muffler. It was Tommy. Tall and gaunt, he looked about as beat up as the old truck he was driving.

"Tommy! So good to see you!" Frank said, walking out on our front porch to greet his young friend.

"It's been a long time. How 'ya been?" Tommy asked, sheepishly.

The two of them settled into the front porch rockers, and I kept them supplied with tuna sandwiches and lemonade. I knew it would mean a lot to Frank to find out how Tommy was really doing.

The better part of the afternoon passed, and I busied myself watering the vegetable garden, then pulled the hose over to the front flower beds by the porch. Spying me there, Frank waved and motioned for me to take the seat next to him. Perhaps Frank thought Tommy need input from a "real" therapist, but I knew the confused boy would benefit much more from a man who cared about him.

"So what are you doing still living at home, Tommy?" Frank picked up their conversation.

"Oh, I don't know. Mom says I can stay as long as I like."

"Hmmm," Frank said. "Is that enough for you?"

"Sure," Tommy said. "She don't like me using drugs, and she kinda puts her foot down about that, but then, I can always sneak around." An unfamiliar, cunning smile spread slowly across the cynical, boy/man's face.

"You've gotten tangled up with drugs, then?" Frank asked.

"Yeah, just minor stuff mainly."

As I listened to the two of them talk, Tommy revealed he'd been in a couple of scrapes with the law, but his mom bailed him out of jail each time. He'd racked up nearly fifteen hundred dollars worth of speeding tickets (driving her car), but she paid them off, because, bless his heart, he didn't have a job. Tommy topped off his story by saying he'd stolen some jewelry from his best friend's mom to get money for drugs. After he pawned the jewelry, the woman pressed charges against Tommy. "This time," he said, "I was really scared." But Tommy begged his mom to save him once again, and she came to the rescue. She bought the jewelry from the pawn shop, returned it to the friend's mother, and the woman dropped the charges.

The Velveteen Woman

Whew! The list of Tommy's disasters was nearly as endless as his mom's list of interventions. But Frank saw beneath the young man's veneer of cynical boasting. Tommy seemed to almost be laughing at his mom, and he'd clearly lost all respect for himself. At the bottom of the pile of disasters was a shame-based identity, years in the making. Tommy had grown up on the outside and gotten pretty rough around the edges, but inside he was still a child, getting tidied up whenever he needed it. And though he accepted her offers of rescue, he secretly hated her manipulations.

Tommy finally finished his story. Frank had been saving his comments until he was done.

"So what now, Tommy?" he asked.

"Dunno."

"Why'd ya come to see me?" Frank probed.

"Not sure. It's just been so long."

"Tommy, you've made a lot of mistakes," Frank said. It was no time to mince words. "I'm gonna give you some advice, son, because that's why I think you came." He cleared his throat, leaned forward and looked Tommy in the eye. "Your life is *your* responsibility, not your mom's. What your life became or becomes is the result of choices—your choices—lined up one after another."

Frank paused, as Tommy shuffled his feet and shifted in his rocking chair. "Son," Frank went on, "it will cost you something to run your own life. But no price is too high to pay. Your life is all you have, and you have to claim it. Why don't you start making some better choices?"

Tommy didn't answer. After a few minutes, Tommy and Frank hugged, and the sad young man with a defeated spirit drove away in his beat up old car. That was a couple of years ago, and we haven't heard from Tommy since. We can't say for sure how he's doing, but the fact that he never came back is not a good sign.

Sometimes, Nana's nursery seems to have so much to offer, we can't see much advantage to moving to life's larger living rooms. Tommy allowed his mom to swoop into his life every time he made a mess because frankly, he got a lot of perks: free meals, a place to stay, no rules. The comfortable misery of the nursery felt too secure to leave. The only thing Tommy had to relinquish was his own self-respect.

It is a fact of life: insecurity attracts lots of Nanas. The more unsure you are that you are a lovable person, precious and unique, the more likely it is you'll allow yourself to be tidied up and told what to do by a Nana. There are plenty of them out there, even among Christians, just waiting to "lord it over" others.

———⚬——— ———⚬———

Madeleine was a single, junior high art teacher. Over lunch one day, she told me about her frustration with her job. "I don't think I have the patience to work with junior high kids," she began. "But I've tried high school already, and I *know* I don't have what it takes to teach young children."

"Madeleine, do you like teaching?" I asked.

"You know, I really don't," she replied hesitantly. "My parents always wanted me to be a teacher, especially my mother. She was a teacher and, after all, she helped finance my education." Madeleine's voice took on a sad tone. "Besides, it's a stable career."

"What is it that you *really want* to do?" I asked.

"Well," Madeleine responded, as her eyes lit up, "I really do love the arts. I've sold my collages in galleries over the past few years, and I'd love to have my own gallery someday."

"But something holds you back. What is it?" I asked.

"My friends say it's not practical," she replied. "And I know that's true. It's *not* practical." Then, thoughtfully, she added, "Yet, when I talk to God about it, He seems to encourage me. I even had a call from a gallery in Santa Fe recently. They're interested in my work!"

Over the next couple of years, Madeleine continued to ask God, "Is this a part of what you have created me to do?" Today, she lives in Santa Fe, New Mexico and owns a gallery in a nearby town. Not only does she display and sell her own work in the gallery, she also designed a line of unique gift cards which are distributed nationwide. When Madeleine stopped looking to others to define who she was, looked inside her own heart, and listened for God's voice, she started to live more authentically, as the person she was created to be.

Although I don't recommend we all walk off from our jobs and find something more interesting and creative to do, it's living the life we were made to live that's important. When we don't assume responsibility to be in charge of our own lives, we're likely to give away our personal power, living under somebody else's control.

Or, assume the role of Nana ourselves.

Dead or Alive

In the late 1800s Henrik Ibsen wrote a play called *Hedda Gabbler*. I became familiar with the play when I worked as secretary to Dean Corrigan at the University of Texas at Dallas. Typing his notes, I came to some understanding of this neurotic, beautiful but bored woman who ended up acting as a Nana, killing the creative life force of others because she could not live the life she herself was called to live.

Near the beginning of the play, Hedda Gabbler married a dull, boring man named George Tesman. She later said she'd married him because she'd "danced herself out" at age twenty-five. In previous days Hedda had been a woman of tremendous passion and authenticity. But suddenly, she decided to marry George in a mysterious attempt to snuff out the embers of her own creative fire, entering into a life that would kill and deaden her soul.

As the story progresses, Hedda falls in love with a wildly innovative literary man who has written a magnificent manuscript about the future, filled with hopes and dreams. But alas, the man is in love with someone else. In retaliation, Hedda decides to burn his manuscripts. "I am killing your child," she says, as she feeds pages of the manuscript into a fire, one at a time. Hedda cannot stand to see authentic life thriving in anyone else while she herself withers inside. In the end, Hedda viciously destroys the man she loves because she cannot bear to see him enjoy the passion she had starved in herself.

There's a bit of Hedda Gabbler in each of us. Like Hedda, if we do not live the life we are called to live, if we are not authentic, we can *become* Nanas ourselves, spinning webs of destruction for others because we are not comfortable in our own Real skin. God meant us to live the life He gave us. When we call the shots for someone else's life, or place ourselves under another's control, we suffer from a Nana complex. Life is confining. Sooner or later, the nursery is found lacking in adventure, and we want out.

WHILE WE HAVE THE GIFT OF LIFE,
IT SEEMS TO ME THE ONLY TRAGEDY
IS TO ALLOW PART OF US TO DIE—
WHETHER IT IS OUR SPIRIT, OUR CREATIVITY,
OR OUR GLORIOUS UNIQUENESS![3]

GILDA RADNER

Like the Skin Horse in the nursery with the Velveteen Rabbit, we need to know what we're made for. But how do we learn that? If focusing on a perfect performance, good looks, comparisons, and getting caught up in a Nana's swoop are roadblocks on the pathway to Real, then how do we get there? How do we become Real?

I am finding that it all begins when we snuggle with the Master. When we crawl into the lap of our Abba Father and stop listening to the distracting noises around us. When we listen for God's voice calling us His beloved. If you are weary of insecurity and emptiness, tired of wandering down rabbit trails and running into dead ends, maybe it's time to return home. To sit quietly. Just you and God. You may find that while you've been out trailblazing, looking for love, it's been with you all along.

Fake Fur
Perception:

An untidy life is unacceptable. If I can't keep my life neat
and manageable, it means I need others to tell me what to do.

Real Skin
Reality:

If I dare to live the authentic life I was created to live, it will be messy
at times, not always tidy. But if I don't live authentically, I run the risk
of losing my zest for life, becoming dull and bored, or susceptible to
every Nana who comes swooping my way.

PART 3

Snuggling
with
the Master

The Skin Horse had lived longer in the nursery than any of the others. He was so old that his brown coat was bald in patches and showed the seams underneath, and most of the hairs in his tail had been pulled out to string bead necklaces.

CHAPTER 8

Skin Horse Mentors

I've heard of people consciously choosing someone as a role model to follow because of character qualities, personal strengths, or talents they possess. I can't say I purposefully sought out a suitable mentor. I think perhaps I was unaware of a mentor's value, and not yet wise enough to know what sort of older, wiser guide I would need. Still, somehow I managed to stumble across a wise Skin Horse's path at the most uncanny and critical times in my life. I'd look up from my book of life lessons, and suddenly help was there, right before my eyes just when I needed it most. Just as the Velveteen Rabbit spent long moonlit hours learning from the Skin Horse, I gleaned wisdom from willing role models who set aside hours beyond their job descriptions to help a less-wise apprentice like me. They began by helping me simply gain enough courage to venture outside the nursery. Occasionally, they'd also point out the sharp edges and corners of my life, those pesky, self-guarding habits that kept me from becoming Real.

Since Jesus is not here on earth with "skin on," how do we begin drawing closer to Him, even daring to spiritually snuggle up in His lap? Many times our intimacy with Christ begins by drawing close to those who have spent some years with Him. Skin Horses have gained wisdom that has withstood the tests of time and trends as they learned, bit by bit, the depth of the Master's love for them. The deeper currents of their souls seem somehow more settled, suggesting they have escaped the busy noise of the world and the checklists for living right. These mature friends, or as some call them, 'spiritual guides,' listen carefully, give us space to wonder and mull things over at our own pace. Offering a safe place for us to explore our thoughts, doubts, and dreams, they avoid rushing to give us the answers. Instead, they guide us into our own discoveries. (You can always tell the difference between a Skin Horse and a Nana. The one reflects love and peace; the other control, judgment, and a lack of love.)

Just as the wise Skin Horse in the nursery became Real because he knew he was loved, a good mentor knows that Real is not something we can become by ourselves. It's not a "pull yourself up by your own rabbit ears" kind of deal. Making connection with others, and with God, are essential. Also, a Skin Horse's own life isn't perfect. There will be some "bald patches" and disappointments in their history and times when they may have felt let down by God. Still, even though some of their seams are showing, they unselfconsciously offer up what they've experienced for the benefit of others.

The Giving Tree

When I decided to go back to school to become a therapist, I didn't even know I'd need a mentor. Knee-deep in the mire of my "faith crisis," God plunked one down right in front of me, in the form of a counseling supervisor. Meeting Charles during my first semester back in school was purely a gift.

As I think back on that year, I am reminded of *The Giving Tree*—a story I once read to my sons when they were small. It's a story about a boy, a tree, and sacrificial giving. The tree lovingly shaded the boy throughout his childhood days. The boy climbed the tree's trunk, swung from his branches, and ate his apples. The boy loved the tree and the tree was happy. As time went by, the boy grew up and went away. But periodically, he came back to visit the tree.

When he grew too old for climbing, the boy needed money. So the tree gave the boy his apples so he could sell them for profit. This, too, made the tree happy. The boy went away again, and when he came back he told the tree that this time, he wanted a house. The tree sacrificially gave up his branches so the boy could build his house. Once again, the tree was happy to give.

Then, the boy went away again. This time, for many months and years. Whey the boy returned, the tree was overjoyed to see him. The boy wasted no time before making another request. "Can you give me a boat?" The Giving Tree gave all he had left—his trunk. The boy made a boat, and sailed away.

Many years later, the boy (now an old man) returned to the Giving Tree. "I wish I had something to give you. I have nothing left," the tree said to the boy. "I'm just an old stump." As it turned out, that's all the old boy wanted—a quiet place to sit and rest. And the tree stump was perfect for sitting and resting upon. And again, the tree was happy.[1]

Skin Horse Mentors

In many ways, Charles was a Giving Tree in my life—inviting me to grow beyond the tiny playground of my fear and insecurity. Giving me seeds of wisdom to encourage me to grow, until one day my own life would bear fruit for others.

"Okay. I'll take you on as an intern. I really hadn't planned on it, but I guess you can start next week." Charles' voice trailed off, ending our phone conversation. I was grateful to find a site close to home for my counseling internship. Charles, *Mr. Rhodes* to the students, was the high school guidance counselor; my assignment was to work under his direction for one semester. Little did I know the treasures I'd gain from this experience. More than instruction on how to score a personality profile or motivate wayward adolescents, I would collect gems of courage and hope for the days ahead.

Brimming with energy, Charles only had time for the important things: helping people. They came in various sizes and shapes, but they were all, or at least most of them, broken or struggling, like myself. My counseling internship allowed me to explore questions plaguing me about the future: *Was I too old to start a new career? Did I have the potential to be a good counselor?*

Each Friday when classes were out, I'd grab a Diet Coke and nestle myself in the fluffy purple cushions on Charles' white wicker office couch. (Decorating the counselor's office with the Fightin' Farmers' purple and white was just one of the ways he displayed school spirit.)

"I'm not sure I have what it takes to finish the counseling program," I once said to him, feeling discouraged. At just a hair past forty, doubts about this new career crept in regularly. "Even if I do finish the coursework, I'm not so sure I'd be any good at counseling."

"You have so much to offer as a therapist," Charles said without a trace of insincerity. "You'll help a lot of people. I can see it now." Inviting me to be all I could be without pushing or manipulating, he believed in me, even at a time when I could not believe in myself.

Ashamed of my "checkered with failure" past, I hadn't been able to reconcile my desire to be a family counselor with the fact that I myself had been divorced. It seemed hypocritical, even blasphemous, to encourage couples to work on keeping their marriages together when I hadn't been able to hold my own first marriage together.

"You don't have to know *everything*," Charles said. "Share with people what you do know. Stop trying to be a perfect example." Less concerned with my fragile feelings than he was with my inability to be authentic, Charles challenged me often during the months I worked at the high school. "There you go again, China Doll," he'd often say when my carefully guarded perfectionism got in the way of relating effectively with a student in need of help. Like a giant magnet, Charles drew to the surface of my awareness all the tiny specks of genuineness he saw deep within me. This was a time in life when God was also sending me a similar message: *Let your life be about Me, not just you. Move over. Make room for My victory in the midst of your failures. Let My wholeness cover your broken, fragmented soul.*

Until this experience, I'd considered it vitally important to always be nice. And there were times when I thought Charles' challenges were not especially nice. But one thing was for sure—he was Real. In much the same way as the Skin Horse explained Real to the Velveteen Rabbit, Charles was more interested in helping people live out their full potential than he was in being nice. Whether it was a student wanting advice about which college to attend or a wanna-be professional counselor in need of self-confidence, Charles had just the right words to appropriately challenge and motivate.

"Give yourself permission to succeed," he said, trying to encourage me. *Give myself permission?* I had to mull that one over. *Hadn't I always tried desperately to succeed? At being a wife? A mother? A Christian? What did he mean?* Over time, I observed Charles interacting with people. Many came to him in need of help, and his golden apples of wisdom fell to the ground. Some people picked them up and ate them gratefully. Others walked on by, leaving them untouched. Charles' part was simply to release the fruit and let it fall. The results were up to others.

During the course of my internship, I gained hope that I too could become a Giving Tree like Charles. But I'd have to make some changes in the ways I related to people and to God. I'd have to stop performing and begin giving from my heart. I'd have to stop holding on, desperately hoarding my own fruit because it was imperfect, and begin releasing it to others around me. I'd have to stop blocking Jesus from caring for others through me.

Skin Horse Mentors

It would take some time for the lessons I learned from Charles to sink in deep enough to make a difference in my life. One evening, months after my internship was completed, I was looking over a passage in the book of Isaiah, and the thought came to me that *Jesus' ministry was not to the strong, but to the poor, the broken-hearted, captives, and prisoners.* If all I could do was connect with people, touch them, identify with them, that would be enough. That would be following His example.

I also noted, as I examined the life of Jesus in the Scriptures, that He was not always nice. But He was always Real. Jesus lived out His life doing things differently. He ate with tax collectors and talked with prostitutes, and the religious leaders, major "Nanas" in His day, did not approve. Yet Jesus was quick to cut through the hypocrisy of the Pharisees as they stood staunchly robed in perfection, carefully keeping the law. Jesus wasn't crucified for being nice. What got Jesus killed was being 100 percent Real.

Charles had been right. I needed to give myself permission to succeed. And to succeed meant to let the fruit of the Holy Spirit fall down from my life for others around me. To be available, to be imperfect, and give what I had to give, this would be enough. Why? Because God is looking for teachable hearts, not perfect performances.

Elisabeth Elliot said "He is in the business of making new men and women. Jesus died that we might no longer live for ourselves. He wants to live His life in us, and thus to make us Life-givers."[2] Isn't that amazing? God wants to show Himself to the world, even through messed up checkered-with-failure lives like mine. And if it's true for me, it's surely true for you too.

Eventually, this passage in Isaiah became a sort of personal counselor's creed for the work I would begin to do with clients, empowered by Jesus:

THE SPIRIT OF THE SOVEREIGN LORD IS ON ME,
BECAUSE THE LORD HAS ANOINTED ME TO PREACH
GOOD NEWS TO THE POOR,
HE HAS SENT ME TO BIND UP THE BROKENHEARTED,
TO PROCLAIM FREEDOM FOR THE CAPTIVES
AND RELEASE FROM DARKNESS FOR THE PRISONERS,
TO PROCLAIM THE YEAR OF THE LORD'S FAVOR
AND THE DAY OF VENGEANCE OF OUR GOD,
TO COMFORT ALL WHO MOURN,
AND PROVIDE FOR THOSE WHO GRIEVE IN ZION—
TO BESTOW ON THEM A CROWN OF BEAUTY
INSTEAD OF ASHES,
THE OIL OF GLADNESS
INSTEAD OF MOURNING,
AND A GARMENT OF PRAISE
INSTEAD OF A SPIRIT OF DESPAIR.

ISAIAH 61:1-3

Like the Giving Tree, Charles continued to share the fruits of his wisdom, to encourage me, and others, to make our own boats and houses. I sailed away with the armload of materials he had given me, ready to build my own boat. As I looked back over my shoulder, I saw him smiling with contentment. And I knew that at any time I might go back for a visit, I could count on finding a quiet place to sit and rest.

BY THEIR FRUIT YOU WILL RECOGNIZE THEM . . .
LIKEWISE EVERY GOOD TREE BEARS GOOD FRUIT . . .

MATTHEW 7:16-17

Do you have a mentor or role model? Someone who reaches out to you with encouragement and motivation? A Skin Horse who listens carefully and calls out the best in you? Perhaps, for you, it won't be a professional mentor, but an older woman you admire. One who embodies character qualities you'd like to develop.

. . . Perhaps a woman like Nell.

Pearls of Grace

The dried leaves crunched on the sidewalk like crispy potato chips beneath my feet as I walked toward the double-wide mobile home. The sky was just beginning to turn orange-red on this late Indian summer afternoon. I'd come to visit Nell, an elderly shut-in.

Knocking on the door, I reminded myself that I didn't have to stay long, just a quick visit. Maybe half an hour to cheer up a lonely old couple.

"Just a minute," Dick called through the glass door. After greeting me he pointed to a place on the couch where I could sit near his wife, who had spent most of her days in a motorized cart since she was stricken with rheumatoid arthritis in her forties.

Piled high at one end of the couch were books on Christian living, World War II, and various other topics. An electric massager lay beside the books with its cord wrapped loosely around it. Part of Dick's daily routine for the past several years had been to massage Nell's deteriorating shoulders to minimize the pain as her bones wasted away. Nell had become literally "loose in the joints" and "bald in patches."

"Tell me how you're doing, and what's going on in your life," Nell began our conversation.

"Oh, fine," I answered. *Now it's my turn to ask how she's doing,* I thought, sighing with dread as I anticipated a long complaintive response.

"No, I mean, tell me what you've been up to," Nell persisted with genuine interest.

"Well, actually I've been a little stressed out," I said, as I accepted her invitation to be Real and dropped my guard. Two-and-a-half hours later I walked out the door of their home. *How was Nell doing?* I wondered with surprise. We'd spent the entire afternoon discussing everything from Sadaam Hussein to wild and hilarious tales about her shaving the legs of girls in a juvenile detention home during her younger years. Even in those days, Nell had the heart of a social worker. She had no idea that shortly after she welcomed God into her life and asked for a ministry she would become immobilized and begin a lifelong vocation of prayer for others.

I couldn't help wondering if Nell had become disillusioned when God's love didn't guarantee her a healthy life, the way I had been disappointed to find that God's love didn't guarantee a happy marriage. Although I was eager to learn more about her, I decided not to ask her all my questions in one day. As I drove away in my car, I found myself wondering when I could find time to come back to this cozy nest for our next chat. I smiled to myself, recalling my pious intentions to cheer this old couple with my effervescent presence, and cherished the happy surprise of simply being Real.

A friendship blossomed between Nell and me. She wanted to know about other people and what was going on in the world. She never wanted to dwell on her pain. Still, I could count on her to give an honest reply when I asked how she was feeling. She was as likely to say "It's hurting like heck today" as "I'm just praising the Lord." But she always ended with "Tomorrow will be another day. Somehow, God's grace gets me through it."

If my idea of a Real woman was once confined to a church building, a prayer list, and a few do's and don'ts, I changed my mind after getting to know Nell. The paradoxes I'd always had trouble accepting as a part of life in a fallen world seemed to come quite naturally to her. Like the psalmist, she believed God, and there were times when she doubted. She praised and she lamented. She had hope and she got discouraged.

As I observed her honest responses to life, I gradually became a little more accepting of my own inconsistencies. In some ways I was free, in other ways I was in bondage. I was genuine, and I still played a lot of games. In the safety of Nell's company, I began to accept paradox as a part of life, and to notice this particularly in the life of Jesus. He became weary, yet He is our rest. He was sold for thirty pieces of silver, and He bought our redemption. He died so we could live. "To seek truth involves an integration of things that seem separate and look like opposites when, in reality, they are intertwined and related in some ways."[3]

By admitting there was a dark side of her, Nell gave others a chance to see God's light and grace in her life. Thomas Merton said, "A saint is not someone who is good but who experiences the goodness of God."[4] Nell's genuineness about who she was made me want to kick off my shoes and put up my feet, resting under the umbrella of her acceptance. I'd notice the muscles in the back of my neck begin to relax as we visited. Before long, I was referring to her as my "Texas Mother."

A thinker and a doer, Nell had not fallen for the myth that to be still and pray is to do nothing. Although she wanted to be physically healed, it had not happened. People in some of the churches she had attended were puzzled and frustrated; they didn't know how to categorize Nell. *Was there unconfessed sin in her life that kept her from getting well? Perhaps she should eat only certain foods. Maybe the doctor hadn't prescribed the right medication.* As years passed, Nell settled into a vocation of prayer for others, counting on God's grace to enable her to bear the intense pain, one day at a time.

"I thought I would feel closest to God when I'm feeling worst and needing Him most, like Mother Teresa did," Nell said one day as she suffered a bout of pneumonia in addition to her usual daily pain quota. "That's not that way it is for me." For Nell, intimacy with God happened as she prayed for others. She poured her heart out to Him on behalf of friends and family, and He blessed her with a deep sense of His comforting presence.

"How's the book coming?" she often asked. "Tell me specifically how I can pray for your writing." Her prayers became a kind of safety net that I counted on when facing a state board exam, a challenging client load, or just the trials of everyday life. Nell often teased that my life would surely be a big mess without all her prayers. We laughed, but I secretly dreaded the day when this faithful saint, who gave me so much that I didn't deserve, would no longer be around. As she reached out and touched me with God's grace, I nestled in a little closer to His heart.

Like Jesus, mentors give us something we cannot pay back. But what we can do is let others' generosity and undeserved gifts move us on to become disciples of grace. We, too, can become Giving Trees. The pertinent question is not *How can I pay my mentors back?* but *How can I turn my indebtedness into gifts for others?*

Nell had lived many years with excruciating pain, yet somehow she learned to put others first, without ever denying the reality of her suffering. She knew she didn't have all the answers. For her, only God was big enough to be God. Nell showed me how to live. And a bit further down the path, she would show me how to die.

. . . But I'll save that story for another chapter.

Fake Fur
Perception:

A good Skin Horse has an exemplary life.
This is what qualifies him or her to be a mentor.

Real Skin
Reality:

Skin Horse mentors offer their life experiences for
the benefit of others. As they pass on the fruit of the Holy Spirit,
their vulnerability and closeness to God
help others see His heart.

But very soon, he grew to like it, for the Boy used to talk to him, and made nice tunnels for him under the bedclothes that he said were like the burrows the real rabbits lived in. And they had splendid games together in whispers.

CHAPTER 9

Whispers of Love

"Here! My mom said I had to show this to you." Thirteen-year-old Connie thrust her report card into my lap at the beginning of her third counseling session. Connie was failing two classes and her other grades had dropped significantly during the previous six weeks grading period. So far, I hadn't made any progress in developing a relationship with her.

"How do you feel about these grades?" I asked.

"I don't know," replied the sullen-faced girl, arms folded.

"What happens now?"

"I'm grounded, and I don't care. It doesn't matter."

Silence.

"Connie, what's going on inside that you need to talk about? What are you so mad about?" I questioned, inviting her to open the locked door to her emotions.

No response. It was as if we were speaking different languages. I couldn't make a connection with her.

Then an idea popped into my head.

"Ever go to the movies?" I asked.

"Some," was her one-word response.

"What kind of movies do you like?" I prodded, hoping to get a conversation started.

"*Poltergeist, Friday the Thirteenth,* and *Halloween,*" Connie replied cynically. If she couldn't maintain her silence, then at least she'd try to shock me.

"What do you like most about those movies?" I went along.

"They're not boring. I like action!"

"What else besides action?" I pressed her.

"I suppose you want me to say I like cutesy movies like *Little Women*. Well, I HATE *Little Women!* People aren't really like that," Connie spat out.

"Then what else *do* you like besides action?" I probed.

"Adventure," Connie said, unfolding her arms, now leaning forward in her chair. "Actually, my favorite movie of all time is *Star Wars*, and I just love Princess Leah."

"Why Princess Leah?" I asked with curiosity. Connie's demeanor softened, but her tone of voice remained aggressive, volatile.

"Because Princess Leah doesn't wait around for *men* to tell her what to do, like my mom does. Princess Leah thinks for herself. Mom's stupid boyfriend tells her to ground me, and so she does. Just because *he* said so!"

"Oh, I see. So you're mad at Mom, and you don't like her boyfriend."

After several failed attempts at communicating, I'd found her "language": movies! Finally, we were on our way to understanding each other.

If we're going to talk meaningfully with others, the way the Boy talked intimately to the Velveteen Rabbit, we'll have to speak a common language. Whether we're trying to talk to each other as friends, in marriage, or in a more formal relationship, the speaker must send messages in ways the listener can hear and understand. Noted author, counselor, and marriage seminar director Gary Chapman says in his book *Five Love Languages* that people use five basic "languages of the emotions" to communicate love to one another: quality time, acts of service, gift giving, words of affirmation, and physical touch. In addition to these basic "languages," Chapman says there are many dialects for effectively expressing love to our spouse. "The number of ways to express love within a love language is limited only by one's imagination. The important thing is to speak the love language of your spouse."[1]

Although it is wise for us to learn to communicate with our spouses in a love language they understand, it's different between God and us. Of course, He doesn't need anybody to teach Him how to communicate with you, but you may need some practice listening for His whispers of love. In these modern times, listening for God's voice has been replaced by "how to" books and manuals. How to study the Bible. How to pray. How to be spiritual. But God knows you, uniquely. He made you. Although books and manuals may be of some use, God alone can tell you "how to" experience intimacy with Him. He knows your love languages. He knows all about your needs, your deepest desires, your most hidden tender spots. With perfect understanding of your nature, He uses a myriad of ways to call you to Himself, creating a longing within your heart that only He can satisfy. We just need to slow down a bit to listen, take some time to watch, to discover the languages and dialects God uses to speak to us.

The Languages of Nature and Music

I WILL WOO HER, I WILL GO WITH HER INTO THE WILDERNESS
AND COMFORT HER . . .

HOSEA 2:14-15 (NEB)

One of the things I love most about living in the country is watching the sun go down. The large atrium window in the back of our kitchen provides a natural picture frame for God to display His paintings in the sky. On a cold, clear winter evening, Frank and I have been known to pull up chairs and watch the sky turn bright yellow-orange just moments after the sun descends beyond the horizon. As the bright orange darkens into orangy-pink, then deepens to a purplish rose, we often just sit side by side and watch the colors change. It wouldn't be exaggerating to say I've been known to shed a few tears when the colors are especially vivid or when, for some unknown reason, God seems especially near. The language of God's love for me personally, often comes in forms of nature. God pursues me through hand-painted horizons, musical breezes, and trickling streams. I can strongly identify with Ken Gire's sentiments in his book, *Windows of the Soul:*

Within our hearts is a longing—a profound cry of the soul for something our theologies can only point us to, never replace. Intimacy with God. Something that has no human or earthly substitute. Yet, if we pause to listen, we will discover how often God speaks to us through human and earthly means. He stands at the windows of the easily overlooked and the unlikely, tapping at the pane. He beckons us to places of encounter where we learn how well he understands the language of our hearts.[2]

In the least likely of places—our backyards and living rooms, at the movie theater, or in a book of poetry—God whispers His love to us and displays His majesty and grace before our eyes in everyday settings, if only we can recognize His language of love. This kind of seeing and hearing are matters of the heart. It is our hearts that respond to the wooing voice of God, rather than our intellect.

Have you ever been hiking on a mountain path and come upon a young fawn that you could barely see at a distance, through the trees and undergrowth, as she silently lapped water from a glassy still pond? Or walking along the beach at sundown and the sea foam mixed with glints of the day's last sun rays looked like mounds of liquid diamonds? Perhaps a memory from childhood flashes through your mind, or a familiar smell wafts by, reminding you of a magic moment from days gone by. At such a time, have you wished for someone close to you to share that special moment with?

Often times we look for God in the magnificent, the mighty, the spectacular. But usually He comes in a gentle whisper, like the Boy having splendid games with the Velveteen Rabbit. We just need to keep looking for Him, listening for Him, learning about the love languages He uses to speak to us.

IT IS BY OUR HEARTS THAT WE KNOW GOD, AND NOT BY REASON.[3]

OSWALD CHAMBERS

The Languages of Music, Dance, and Dreams

Diedra, a client who once dreamt of becoming a professional skater, told me of a time when God's gentle presence beckoned to her. It was a Saturday night, and her husband had to work. For some reason, Diedra was feeling lonely. No matter how hard she tried to center her mind on positive thoughts, a heavy sadness prevailed. She dimmed the lights and lit some candles, trying to welcome herself into her own home. "Oh well, I'll do some reading," she said out loud. One last attempt to lift her own spirit. But the warmth of contentment refused to settle in.

Thoughts of her dad, whom Diedra still missed twenty-five years

The *Velveteen Woman*

after his death, flooded her mind. She recalled memories of playing in her dad's rose garden when she was about five or six years old. Lying on her tummy, she would float her miniature china dolls down the rose garden river on mulberry leaf-boats. Neither little Diedra nor her dad would talk. She felt nurtured just being near her kind, gentle father. But now all she had was a sister, who lived far away in another state. Even her mother was gone. Diedra's heart yearned for family. For familiarity. For someone close in heart to connect with.

It must have been those dancing patterns of filtered sunlight that suggested to Diedra, even at the young age of five or six, that there must be something more to this life—something transcendent. Someplace beyond her dad's rose garden, where she would one day be complete. Someplace called Home. Where she will never again feel lonely. Tonight she longed for Home.

Opening a book, Diedra snuggled into her cozy rocking chair. Her eyes raced across the pages, but she didn't know what the words said. She tried again to concentrate, but it was no use. She closed the book. *Maybe this is a good time to try out the new tape my sister sent,* she mused. Perhaps it would at least be a way to connect with a loved one. Several songs played as Diedra sat in her blue swivel rocker, listening to the piano notes go by. And then, a poignant, haunting song began. She checked the tape jacket and saw that the tune was called "Until the Last Moment." As Diedra listened to the piano, joined by violins and cellos, a mysterious feeling swept over her. She became aware of a warm, welcoming presence, perhaps not unlike the one that had first convinced me of God's smile that spring day on my back deck.

The melody called to Diedra, enticed her, as if to say, "Come, let's dance." She decided to let herself be drawn into the mystique of the moment. And even to dress for the occasion. *Why not?* Although her dream of becoming a professional skater had not come true, she'd often said that when she got to heaven, she looked forward to wearing a beautiful, flowing costume to wear as she skated and danced gracefully before her King.

To enter into the mood, Diedra went to the bedroom bureau drawer and withdrew an old black dance leotard. She slipped into it and then pulled her hair back, clipping it into a ponytail. Looking into the bathroom mirror, she checked herself. *Oh yes, sparkly dangly earrings would be nice too. And red lipstick to add a final touch.*

The slow, dramatic melody beckoned to Diedra again, calling her to a moment of sacred intimacy. A moment she could only experience alone. *Is this the aloneness I was dreading?* she wondered, beginning to relish the mysterious enticement. Then, feeling no less graceful than Katarina Witt herself (Diedra's favorite ice skater because of the emotional depth she exudes as she skates), Diedra began to sway with the music. Somehow she didn't feel alone anymore. As the piano notes ran up and down the keyboard, she skipped across the room, back arched, like a little girl running along the seaside. Then she stopped, raised her arms, and bent at the waist. First to the right, then to the left, slowly. As the finale approached, she bowed deeply, dramatically, worshipfully.

As I listened to Diedra tell her story, visions of Mary of Bethany came to mind. This was the woman who poured a costly flask of oil over Jesus' head just before His burial. It was this same Mary, the sister of Martha, who sat at Jesus' feet listening to Him, responding to Him from her heart, devoting her time and attention to Him. Just being with Jesus. Perhaps Diedra was trying to offer a passionate response to God in a similar way—to answer a message sent in love languages of music and dance—His call for a companion for the evening. That Saturday night, Diedra danced a dance of gratitude, worship, longing, attempting to say "yes" to God's call of love. *I long for You, Lord Jesus. I want You. Come quickly.*

Jesus had called Diedra into His presence. Not because she sought Him. Because He is a loving pursuer who whispers His passionate affection to us in love languages and dialects as numerous as the grains of sand on the beach. He had pursued Diedra's company through a longing for her father, and memories of his sunlit rose garden. Through piano chords and strains of violin music—a gift from her sister. Later that night, Diedra went to sleep and dreamt, not of becoming a professional skater, but of her Dad's funeral. It was a sleep of enchantment, as yet another of God's love languages, the dialect of sweet dreams, kissed her resting thoughts. When she awoke the next morning she could almost smell the rose petals she had sprinkled over her dad's grave so many years ago, her way of saying "farewell for now."

"Perhaps it was a family night after all," Diedra said, closing her story.

The Language of Childhood Remembered

Max Lucado has written a wonderful little book called *Just in Case You Ever Wonder*.[4] It's a children's book actually, but I often read it to women and adolescent girls during a counseling session. We never outgrow our need to hear that we are absolutely precious and cared for by God. Through this little book, God has often talked to women in a language they have understood for a long, long time—the language of childhood remembered. Linda is one of these women.

Whispers of Love

Linda was beautiful, inside and out. Even so, her heart was aching for love and acceptance. Emotionally frayed, she had come for counseling because she'd had an affair.

After trying several ways to help Linda begin to understand her insecurities, I finally resorted to simplicity, hoping to get across a profound truth: God loves you unconditionally.

"Linda, I want to read this little book to you," I said. "Try to just let yourself hear the words, even though it's a children's book. There's a message here for grown-ups, too."

"Long, long ago God made a decision—a very important decision. He made the decision to make you." I began the story.

"He made you in a very special way. God made you like no one else," I said, turning the page. Looking up, I detected the magical disarming of defenses that so often occurs when we hear children's stories. Sadly, some unwritten rule dictates that we should no longer read them to ourselves once we're "mature."

Going on, I read, "If you looked all over the world—in every city in every house—there would be no one else like you . . . " That's as far as I got in the story that day.

"God loves *me*? I want to believe it. Can it be true?" she asked through tears. Somehow, in the simplicity of childhood language, words about God's hugs and protection reached out to Linda and extended hope. Called to her in such a way that she began to get the message she was loved. Whispered to her that God's angels were always watching over her. Oh yes, even her.

"It has been said that faith is 'a certain widening of the imagination.' When Mary asked the angel, 'How shall these things be?' she was asking God to widen her imagination."[5] Linda came to believe that something beyond her comprehension could actually be true. God loved a woman like her. To Mary, God spoke through an angel. To Linda, He whispered His message through a children's storybook. Imagine that!

Whispers of Reel Love

God can inspire us through music, nature, books, and poems. As we saw with Connie, the angry adolescent at the beginning of this chapter, *movies* can be another vehicle for communication between our heart and God's. A way of widening our imagination, opening up reality, mirroring moments of Real life, and reflecting human nature to increase our faith or crystallize moments of truth. We identify with the characters. Our hearts go out to them because they are like us. They struggle as we do. As we see little vignettes of life played out before our eyes at the movies, if we have ears to hear and eyes to see, we may encounter God's voice calling intimately to us.

Recently, I was discussing the movie *The Horse Whisperer* with a friend. He said that in most movies, he finds a Christ figure—a character who represents some quality embodied by Jesus. He went on to explain that in *The Horse Whisperer*, a movie about a rancher named Tom Booker who helps wounded and traumatized horses by gaining their trust and understanding their ways, he saw such a Christ figure.

"You'd think it would be Tom Booker," my friend said, "because he encourages Annie to be faithful to her husband. But I think the Christ figure in this movie is actually Annie's husband, Robert." I confessed I hadn't been as keen an observer as my friend. Now curious, I returned to the movie theater for a second viewing.

In the movie, Annie and Robert's daughter, Grace, is involved in a catastrophic accident, in which she loses her best friend and part of her leg all at once. As if that weren't enough, Grace's beloved horse, Pilgrim, is critically injured. Grace seems to have no will to live, no reason to go on. Desperate to help her daughter find hope, Annie locates a Horse Whisperer, someone who understands that the relationship between man and beast has been fragile from the beginning of time, who knows how to tend an animal's wounds.

Annie and Grace take Pilgrim to the Booker Ranch while Robert remains in New York taking care of business. As they watch Tom Booker tenderly relating to Pilgrim, Annie begins to discover unexpected, simple pleasures on the ranch. Peaceful suppers in front of a family hearth, spirited rides on horseback in Tom's company. An emotional attraction grows into unsolicited feelings of love. When Robert arrives at the ranch unannounced, Annie is forced to decide what she wants—her marriage, or a life with Tom on the Booker Ranch.

In a scene near the end, the emotionally torn Annie helps her husband, Robert, prepare to return home with Grace, saying she'll follow in a few days. "I could use the time alone," she says. "It's not like I don't know the way home." I noted Robert's poignant response which, in the end, won me over to my friend's view that Robert's character was Christlike.

Whispers of Love

"Take your time. I always knew I loved you more." Robert tells her how he has loved her for a long, long time, that everything he did was for her, even promotions in his job were only to better his life with her, that somehow it didn't really matter that they didn't love each other just the same. Then Robert adds, "You don't know if you want a life with me anymore. The truth is, I don't want you to come home until you do know, one way or the other."

Here, Robert is not nice, but Real. His lines convey in an imaginative way, sentiments Jesus expresses to us: *I want you. All of you. I want your whole heart. You were made for Me and nobody else. You are either with Me or against Me.* Likewise, Jesus often has greater purposes in mind for us, even though they are far beyond our comprehension. When we are disappointed or hurt, it looks to us as if He's withholding a blessing, but it's just that God is after our hearts.

We all chase after other loves at times. But He wants us for Himself. He loves us the most, more than we can ever love Him. Still if we don't want to come home He won't force us against our will.

Just as the Velveteen Rabbit became more Real as the Boy talked to him in special ways, playing splendid games together in whispers, so do we grow more Real as God sends messages of love to us. He tirelessly pursues through the Scriptures, through nature, poems, books, and movies, through music, dance, dreams, and memories. Although we often expect to hear from God in the spectacular, most often He speaks to us in gentle ways. In soft whispers.

S-h-h-h.

Listen.

Can you hear Him?

Fake Fur
Perception:

The Scriptures are the only valid way God can communicate
with His people.

Real Skin
Reality:

God uses a myriad of ways, all in alignment with the Scriptures,
to whisper messages of love to those who will but hear and see.
As we hear God speaking to us, day by day, we become more Real.

And for many nights after, the Velveteen Rabbit slept in the Boy's bed. At first he found it rather uncomfortable, for the Boy hugged him very tight, and some times he ... could scarcely breathe ... When the Boy dropped off to sleep, the Rabbit would snuggle down close under his little warm chin and dream, with the Boy's hands clasped close round him all night long. Nana had gone away to her supper and left the nightlight burning on the mantelpiece.

CHAPTER 10

Snuggle in the Struggle

Melanie's stream of built-up agony began with the quiet pitter-patter of a few teardrops. She had come to my office seeking refuge. Soon her tears progressed, like a violent Texas thunderstorm, into raging sobs. Melanie's husband had left home. There were hints of an affair. Her oldest son's graduation from the S.M.U. law school was two weeks away, and Melanie was trying to pull herself together to make last-minute preparations for a post-graduation party.

Just as the Velveteen Rabbit snuggled down close under the Boy's chin at night, Melanie prayed throughout the days, longing to feel God's reassuring comfort when her family fell apart.

"This is supposed to be a happy time," Melanie said, as tears quivered in the corners of her eyes. "How can I go to my son's graduation and smile like everything is just fine? And what if my husband brings his girlfriend to the ceremony?" I simply listened, giving space for Melanie to sort through the rubble of her confusion and despair. "Do you know what I'd really like to understand?" she asked, her face wet with tears. "Where is God in all of this?"

The writer of Psalm 88 knew exactly how Melanie felt:

> WHY, O LORD, DO YOU REJECT ME
> AND HIDE YOUR FACE FROM ME?

FROM MY YOUTH I HAVE BEEN AFFLICTED AND
CLOSE TO DEATH;
I HAVE SUFFERED YOUR TERRORS AND AM IN
DESPAIR.
YOUR WRATH HAS SWEPT OVER ME;
YOUR TERRORS HAVE DESTROYED ME.
ALL DAY LONG THEY SURROUND ME LIKE A
FLOOD;
THEY HAVE COMPLETELY ENGULFED ME.
YOU HAVE TAKEN MY COMPANIONS AND
LOVED ONES FROM ME;
THE DARKNESS IS MY CLOSEST FRIEND.

PSALM 88:14-18

As Melanie cried and blew her nose, and cried some more as she made a mound of wet, wadded-up Kleenex on the couch beside her, I resisted my impulse to assuage her grief. I just sat with her as she wept. And wept. Near the end of our session, my brain made a quick but thorough scan to see if I didn't have *something* cataloged away *somewhere*— in my therapist's "Emergency" file—some kind of holy quick fix to lighten her load.

Nothing.

Then, Melanie's lament came to an end. The emotional storm was over. At least for now. A turbulent wave of tears had been sent to cleanse her soul of today's portion of pain. With eyes still glistening, she reached out for a hug, then left my office.

Why is it so difficult to just sit with someone in despair? To be with them in their pain and confusion? After Melanie had gone, my mind wandered back to a time years ago when I felt like Melanie. A time when I needed someone to just be with me in my sorrow.

My dad had just died of cancer at fifty-eight, and oh, what a loss this was to me. It was one of those *Where is God in all of this?* moments. Several of my good friends attended his funeral. I recall that my best friend, Ruthie, walked up to me at the burial site, looked me in the eyes, and we both cried, and hugged, and cried some more. Then, Ruthie put her hands on my shoulders and our eyes locked in a comforting and reassuring gaze I shall never forget. Without ever speaking a word, she walked away.

That loving gaze from my best friend comforted me beyond words. Somehow I knew that she missed my dad too, and that it was okay to mourn. We grieved together and a little bit of healing took place. Remembering the strength I drew from Ruthie's presence that day gave me some consolation that just *being with* Melanie was enough on a day like today. Just sitting with her and offering my presence as she grieved. No need to preach a sermon on joy. Not today.

Snuggle in the Struggle

Sometimes when we are most desperate for quick relief, we get out our trusty box of holy Band-Aids and slap them over gaping wounds. A pretty, pink placebo for emotional cancer. We quickly suck it up and "turn it over to the Lord." But, as John Powell has said, "When you repress or suppress those things which you don't want to live with you don't really solve the problem because you don't bury the problem dead—you bury it alive. It remains alive and active inside you."[1] Trusting God means not to suck it up, but to pour it all out to God.

I don't know about you, but I've done it both ways. There have been times when I snuggled up to God and poured out the contents of my heart; at other times I've turned away from Him in favor of pretentious religiosity. Sometimes He came to me in a way I could sense His presence when I cried out in the dark; at other times He seemed to turn a deaf ear. The best I can do is offer myself to Him, whatever my emotional state, whatever His immediate response.

Jesus is our supreme example of turning to God with His genuine emotions. He didn't pretend to be who He wasn't. In the Garden of Gethsemane, just before He was crucified, Jesus told His disciples, "This sorrow is crushing my life out."[2] Then He turned toward God in prayer and said, "My Father, if there is any way, get me out of this. But please, not what I want. You, what do you want?"[3]

Just as Jesus wanted His disciples to be *with Him* emotionally during His moment of greatest agony, we want someone just to be present with us when we're struggling. And like the disciples who fell asleep, we find ways to escape the agony of emotional presence because it's so difficult to tolerate the uncomfortableness of not feeling safe, not having the guarantees we want.

Sometimes we have to wait for God. During the darkest nights, we often can't see, feel, or hear Him. We find no evidence of Him in our life situations. Even when we've turned toward Him, cried out to Him, sought Him through the Scriptures, it's as if He's dropped off to sleep, like the Boy in the story.

The Velveteen Woman

As we resist the impulse to apply pious quick fixes, and instead turn our despair Godward, we hang out a welcome sign for Jesus, inviting Him into the living rooms of our inmost being. An open heart and a receptive spirit are diamonds in the mud of suffering.

God may not come quickly when we call. Our hearts may ache. Although He may be there, we can't see Him through our tears and fears.

But the morning is sure to come.

YOU HAVE SEEN ME TOSSING AND
TURNING THROUGH THE NIGHT.
YOU HAVE COLLECTED ALL MY TEARS
AND PRESERVED THEM IN YOUR BOTTLE!

PSALM 56:8 (TLB)

God Can Handle Our Anger, Doubt, and Confusion

Our good friends, Sandra and Fred, sat in shocked silence when the pastor of their large metropolitan church announced he was leaving the ministry because he was involved in the proverbial "affair with the secretary." Determined to find a church where "this kind of thing" wouldn't happen again, Sandra and Fred carefully selected a smaller church—one that sported a firm structure and clear-cut rules. At first, their new environment felt safe, in the same way a strict daddy makes a child feel secure with rigid behavioral limits. When the pastor asked Sandra to be his secretary, she was flattered, and eagerly agreed.

But after a few months, Sandra and her husband began to notice that nearly all of the sermons focused on God's wrath and anger. Hearing the pastor portray God as heavy-handed and punishing, Sandra was fast losing sight of the loving God she once knew and longed to know more deeply. The pastor labored over sermons from one book, Deuteronomy, for a year and a half! Weary from one-sided, law-touting sermons, and thirsty for a word about God's love, even a tiny drop to slake her parched throat, Sandra worked up the courage to ask the pastor when he planned to move on to another topic. The stern taskmaster informed her that the congregation's greatest need was to learn the laws of God, and he wasn't even close to a stopping place. A quiet anger began to simmer just below the surface of Sandra's psyche. Although she was aware of her feelings, she purposed to keep doing her job, avoid conflict with the pastor, and mentally tiptoe around her angry, sleeping giant of a God so He wouldn't get upset.

Snuggle in the Struggle

"I need to have a talk with you, Sandra," the pastor said one day. She cringed. Sandra could feel the tension in her shoulders as she sat down in his office chair.

"I understand you want Margaret to go on a women's retreat," he said in a scolding tone.

"I thought," Sandra began her explanation, then nervously paused to clear her throat. "I thought it might help Margaret's depression if she met some women friends."

"What kind of wives want to be away from their husbands at night?" the pastor asked.

Like a bad little girl getting a scolding, Sandra shrank in her seat, sitting quiet and still as he told her she was out of order because godly wives didn't behave in such ways.

"You make trouble. For a woman, you think too much," he sarcastically dismissed her.

Livid, Sandra resigned her position. She had taken a sizable salary cut to assume this "ministry" position and held in her anger as long as she could. Though she continually cautioned herself against talking disrespectfully to God, bitterness hovered near the surface.

Finally, Sandra and her husband announced they were leaving the little church. "What right do you have to leave?" some admonished them. "That should be the elders' decision!" Others gave them lists of Bible verses as evidence of their sin in leaving.

Sound a bit cultish? Today, this kind of behavior in churches is recognized as a type of spiritual abuse. The reigning philosophy is: Shame people for thinking for themselves, and struggling, until they conform to your norms. Soon they will feel bad and wrong, and then they'll do whatever you tell them to do. It's the same old "shame game" that's been going on for centuries in families. Sadly, it happens in church families too.

Needless to say, Sandra's anger grew to unrighteous proportions when she turned away from God instead of toward Him with her honest feelings. "How can I trust God when His people keep letting me down?" she asked, confused.

I SAID
THIS DESERT LAND IS BARREN
VOID OF LIFE AND BEAUTY.
I DRIVE FOR MILES
SEE NOTHING
ONLY SAND AND SAGE
FEEL NOTHING
ONLY WIND AND HEAT
TASTE NOTHING
BUT SPIT DRIED SPIT.
HE SAID
HAVE YOU EVER DRIVEN
IN SPRING
THROUGH THIS SAME DESERT
SEEN BLOSSOMS FLOWER
GORGEOUS WILD?
IT'S ALL A THING OF TIMING.
SEEDS OF BEAUTY
ARE THERE NOW HIDDEN
WAITING FALL OF RAIN
TO BRING THEM LIFE.
LORD SEND RAIN
UPON MY WORLD
MY LIFE
I'M TIRED OF DRIED SPIT.[4]

JOSEPH BAYLY

Finally, after several months of wandering through the desert of spiritual dryness, Sandra dared to pray again. "I bravely told God all about my anger, and to my amazement, He listened!" Sandra told me as we sat talking at the local yogurt shop. "I mean, I confessed my Real feelings—the sin of my resentment—told Him all about it. I also told Him I didn't feel safe, I felt betrayed by Him, and that I didn't understand His ways."

When Sandra finally let God into her desert experience—when she turned toward Him instead of away from Him with her struggle— God's reassuring love began to calm her angry, unforgiving spirit. Unlike the dead religiosity practiced in the small church, Sandra found freedom in God's living Word. At last, she was becoming Real, finding comfort in God's acceptance, the Oasis she had been searching for all along.

Snuggle in the Struggle

ARE YOU TIRED? WORN OUT? BURNED OUT ON RELIGION? COME TO ME. GET AWAY WITH ME AND YOU'LL RECOVER YOUR LIFE.

MATTHEW 11:28 (TM)

Turn on the Night Light

When the Velveteen Rabbit snuggled up to the Boy as he dropped off to sleep, Nana would leave the night light burning on the mantelpiece. We, too, need a night light. Although God is with us in our darkness, we may not be aware of His presence. We may not be able to feel, touch, or hear Him. We remember His presence before we dropped off to sleep and the nightmares began. We know that we'll see Him again in the morning. It's just making it through the night that can be so difficult.

───────

It was during one of the most painful times of my life that God met me in the private chambers of my heart. Although I could not convince Him to change the painful situation around me, He entered into my deep sorrow. At first, there were no words. Only tears. It would be a long time before I would realize the beautiful, lasting gift He would bring to my soul as a result of those long night hours with Him.

It had been a year and a half since my divorce was finalized. The boys and I had somehow managed to pick up the slivers of our shattered lives and go on. Scott and Brent both had restored their relationships with their dad. Then came the deathblow. Scott had just turned fifteen. His dad wanted him to come and live at his house, but the final decision was left to me. My initial thought: Sounds easy enough—*just* say *"NO."* (However, Scott's dad and I had both seen signs that Scott needed more male influence.) Outbursts of anger, a normal reaction from a boy grieving for his lost family, were beyond my control as I struggled in an already weakened state to survive the emotional earthquake of a family breakup. My energy went into things like buying gas for the car and paying the mortgage. When I came home at night, I had very little left over to offer.

Though I despised the bitter thought of letting Scott go, I could not be what he needed most, at that time in his life. It grew clearer that if he could only live with one of his parents, he'd be better off with his dad. As the days went by, there seemed to be no choice.

"Scott," I said one night over my untouched plate of spaghetti, "your dad wants you to come live with him." *Perhaps he'll protest*, I silently hoped, half holding my breath.

"Oh. Okay," was Scott's trance-like reply. A look of confused ambivalence crossed his face. I'd been right. Scott didn't want to hurt my feelings; he just wanted more of Dad. Actually, he wanted us both, but since he could only have one . . . The piercing pain of family devastation stabbed a little deeper—to the very core of my already wounded heart. *How would I live without my Scotty? How would Brent survive without his brother? How could God allow this complete shredding of our once intact family?*

Scott moved his belongings to his dad's house, and we hugged each other good-bye. *It's the best thing for him,* I consoled myself. It took a while, a few months, before I could really let myself experience the loss. I didn't want to talk about it—not even to God. It was so dark and scary, I didn't dare. However, it was in this midnight hour that God turned on a night-light in my life with Him. In an odd way, it was as if the pain of missing Scott overtook my fear that God didn't really love me. So I took a wild chance. I opened my heart to Him, just a little bit, and in turn, He planted a seed of trust.

As I sat down to pray, it didn't seem enough to just say, "I know you're in control, and that you'll take care of Scott, so please bless him today." I needed more. I needed a deeper awareness of releasing my burden of pain into Gods hands. A thought came to mind. Before I began my prayer, I held out my hands to Jesus, palms up, to signify surrendering my son. Somehow this helped demonstrate to myself the relinquishment, the handing over to God. For me, it made the process more Real. I began to cry. Then, words slowly arose from the floor of my heart. "Oh God. I miss my son! Do You have any idea how much it hurts to let him go?"

Well, of course, God was well acquainted with the sorrow of letting His Son go—His Son, who would be cut off from heaven's home, brutally marred, more than any other man.[5] But the awesome thing I discovered about God was this: my loss, though it looked like a grain of sand on the beach compared to His—was all I could bear. And it was of *great significance* to God. I believed He was listening to me with unmatched tenderness and compassion.

In the dark silence of my prayers, I began to feel comforted. Each day I set aside a half hour to just sit and cry and hold out my hands—palms up—to God. "I place Scott in your arms. He's wounded, so please take good care of him, because I can't." More time passed. I pictured Jesus lovingly taking my son's limp, wounded body from me. It helps me to envision a biblical truth in my mind. So, as I cast all my anxiety on Jesus, remembering His care for me, I pictured myself picking up Scott in my arms (somehow his taller-than-me body was manageable) and carrying him to Jesus. As I cried, Jesus held my son, rocking him, caring for him, holding him close, and then Jesus walked away with him.

Day after day, I envisioned God's care for my son. He could watch over him when I could not. He could be present for Scott when I could not. Some days I didn't want to let Scott go. So I'd cling to his body for a little while. *God, help me open my hands.* I'd cry some more. Jesus waited. As soon as I could, I'd hand Scott over to Jesus and watch them walk away together. I told Jesus how my heart ached when I didn't get to host Scott's sixteenth birthday party. How I missed being the one to send out his high school graduation announcements. How I longed to talk with him over breakfast on the mornings after basketball games and dates. Although I got to watch all his games, I wanted to play a bigger part in his life—a mother's part. I told God how much I missed *living with* my son, even though I did get to see him in the school hallway each day. (I was the headmaster's secretary at his school.)

More days passed. Each day I cried and prayed, palms up, surrendering what I could not change or control and placing it in God's hands. Each day I felt more comforted, more assured that Scott was lovingly cared for. My prayers became simpler. "He's Yours. Please take care of him. I'm Yours. Please take care of me." In time, my heart healed. For the most part, that is. Although I can never regain the years I lost with my son, the essence of our love only grew stronger.

"Mom, you've helped me so much. I don't think I would have made it without you," Scott said to me very recently after resolving a job conflict. "You're my mom, my friend, and my advisor. I love you so much!" (And if you think that won't make a mom's heart swell with joy, well, you'd better think again.)

The day did come when I realized that God had been there in the terror of the dark night, experiencing my grief with me. Even though I could not feel Him, touch Him, or hear Him, He was with me when I was afraid, lonely, and in need of comfort. Like the Velveteen Rabbit snuggling down close under the Boy's chin, I found that God's hands had been clasped close round me throughout my nightmarish agony.

WEEPING MAY REMAIN FOR A NIGHT, BUT
REJOICING COMES IN THE MORNING.

PSALM 30:5

THOU HAS NOT THAT, MY CHILD, BUT THOU HAS ME,
AND AM NOT I ALONE ENOUGH FOR THEE?
I KNOW IT ALL, KNOW HOW THY HEART WAS SET
UPON THIS JOY WHICH IS NOT GIVEN YET.

AND WELL I KNOW HOW THROUGH THE WISTFUL DAYS
THOU WALKEST ALL THE DEAR FAMILIAR WAYS,
AS UNREGARDED AS A BREATH OF AIR,
BUT THERE IN LOVE AND LONGING, ALWAYS THERE.

I KNOW IT ALL; BUT FROM THY BRIER SHALL BLOW
A ROSE FOR OTHERS. IF IT WERE NOT SO
I WOULD HAVE TOLD THEE. COME, THEN, SAY TO ME,
MY LORD, MY LOVE, I AM CONTENT WITH THEE.[6]

AMY CARMICHAEL

Fake Fur
Perception:

God does not approve of me when I feel angry, doubtful, fearful.
These negative emotions are harmful and separate me from God.

Real Skin
Reality:

He can handle our honesty and wants to light the way
through our dark nights.

Spring came, and they had long days in the garden, for wherever the Boy went the Rabbit went too. He had rides in the wheelbarrow, and picnics on the grass, and lovely fairy huts built for him under the raspberry canes behind the flower border.

CHAPTER 11

Picnics on the Grass

Eureka Springs.

Just the sound of the words brings a smile to my face. This little Victorian village nestled in the Ozark mountains has come to be a favorite getaway for Frank and me. Eureka means "I have found it!" As its name suggests, it is the site of natural hot springs bubbling up from deep beneath the surface of the ground. For us, Eureka is a picnic on the grass. A place of reconnecting with the deeper springs of life, with ourselves, each other, and God. A sort of home away from home, where every day is an adventure, food is created and enjoyed as the masterpiece of the day, and simple life is elevated to an art form.

In Eureka, we spend most of our time walking, eating, and visiting with the local folks, who take great delight in sharing their art, creative ideas, and just getting to know each other. Simple pleasures are the highlight of the day—the soft strumming of a six-string guitar, browsing through trinkets at a garage sale, raiding a church bake-off, or just smelling the aroma of spicy Italian sausage mixed with oregano outside Ermilio's Restaurant.

What are some of your ways of "spending long days in the garden" with God, just enjoying the pleasure of His company? Do you think it's important to intentionally *enjoy* Jesus during the good times, or does this seem self-indulgent to you? Many people I know feel unproductive or guilty, scolding themselves if they just kick back, relax, and soak in the joy of God's presence. I once did, too. I had a need to show some sort of "outcome" or "product" for time I spent with God. A completed Bible study, a meal cooked for a neighbor, a prayer list with check marks beside the requests.

The Velveteen Woman

But I am discovering that "picnicking" with God, basking in the pleasure of His company from my heart's inner springs all the way down to the tips of my toes is a vital part of spiritual life. Such "unproductive" moments can even be the times when we come closest to obeying the command to love God with all our hearts (feelings), minds (intellect), and souls (being).[1] I have a feeling that when we get to heaven, we'll be spending lots of long, pleasurable days in the garden with Jesus. But even now, a part of loving God and becoming more Real is welcoming Him into our happy moments, having fun together, and making celebrations out of simple things.

Celebrate the Ordinary

> BUT I FEAR, LEST SOMEHOW . . . YOUR MINDS MAY BE CORRUPTED
> FROM THE SIMPLICITY THAT IS IN CHRIST.
>
> 2 CORINTHIANS 11:3 (NKJV)

Do you ever get up early just to watch the sun come up? If you're not a morning person by nature, this may be nauseating to you. But if you're so inclined, try it. It's certainly not every morning that I rise before the sun, but on those rare days when I do, I love to watch the golden rays of light pierce a dense canopy of leaves and slant their way through the uplifted arms of our native Texas pecan trees. The beams form golden shafts of light that seem almost tangible.

Do you ever just open your front door on a cool morning, put on some music, and read a psalm aloud just to celebrate the new day? Even if you are in the midst of a painful emotional struggle, try injecting your day with some "shots" of joy. Centering your thoughts on positive, scriptural truths can go a long way toward emotionally strengthening you for the day, and lifting your mood.

In the Bible, Jesus said Mary of Bethany paid attention to the most important part of life—living in the present moment and experiencing His presence. We can follow Mary's example by exploring ways to rediscover spontaneity, serendipity, passionately celebrating everyday experiences.

Picnics on the Grass

All of us find different veins of creativity. We don't need to express ourselves in the same ways. In fact, life would be rather dull if we did. While I am easily enamored with nature, music, and art, I enjoy learning ways some other people find nurturing for their souls and intimate pleasures with Christ in everyday life. My friend Sarah likes to grind wheat to make bread for her family. I've known many occasions when she's shared a loaf of bread and a pot of homemade vegetable soup with a friend or neighbor. Finely attuned to the domestic arts, Sarah can arrange some fruit in a pretty bowl in such a way it becomes an invitation to live holistically, heartily, healthily. Sipping freshly squeezed lemonade on Sarah's front porch with a friend offers as much refreshment to her soul as an evening at the symphony does for mine. And then there's Betti Lu, a woman who milks the pleasure of God's company out in the pasture, tending baby calves and training highly spirited quarter horses.

While I admire Sarah and Betti Lu, I am quite different from them. Most of the ways I find to creatively experience God's presence don't yield any outcome at all. Not even a loaf of bread. But I am discovering the value of intangible experiences. They're a lot like taking "soul vitamins." You don't necessarily see any immediate results, but you get healthier and feel better afterward. I now find joy in loving God with my heart and soul as well as with my mind, sometimes "wasting" hours on end just enjoying the pleasure of His company.

WE DO NOT NEED TO ITEMIZE THE CHRISTIAN LIFE,
IT IS ENOUGH TO SEE JESUS . . . EACH ASPECT OF CHRISTIAN
EXPERIENCE IS MADE REAL IN US JUST BY SEEING HIM.[2]

ROY & REVEL HESSION

Professional counselors' conferences can be very inter-

The   esting, but also exhausting. Even when the speakers are moti-

Velveteen vating and full of great ideas, one can get antsy sitting

Woman   through all those meetings, one after another. Eleanor, a fel-

low therapist, found herself in such a state of tired boredom while at a conference on eating disorders we attended recently. As Eleanor wandered through the hotel gift shop during a two-hour lunch break, a kind and attentive shopkeeper suggested she walk to the park just about a half mile down the road. Grateful for the advice, she set out to find some amusement and food.

As Eleanor entered the park, she could hear squeals of children's laughter at a distance. Rounding the corner and passing some neatly groomed hedges, she saw about ten children ranging in age from maybe two to ten, decked out in cutoffs and bathing suits, playing in a row of water fountains. As the streams of water squirted up, the children ran through the liquid shafts, sat on the water spouts, even stuck their faces in the fast-flowing sprays.

Spying a sandwich shop behind the fountains, Eleanor scurried inside, ordered a chicken salad sandwich and a Diet Coke, and glanced over her shoulder to see if the park bench by the children was still empty. *I'll just sit and watch the kids play while I eat my sandwich*, she thought, savoring the break from professional sophistication. As she was on her way to the front door, she had to pass by the goodie counter. (You know, they always put the sweetest temptations right beside the check-out.) "What kind of cookies are THOSE?" Eleanor asked the clerk, eyeing a row of saucer-sized confections topped with generous globs of creamy frosting.

"Carrot cake," the clerk replied.

"Carrot cake *cookies?*" Eleanor asked. Already, she was finding more amusement than she'd expected.

"Oh yeah," the clerk said. "They're our specialty."

"I'll take one of those," Eleanor asserted, with eyes as big as the saucer-sized cookies. "And a peppermint pinwheel lollipop too."

With her mound of treats, she made her way to the park bench outside, near the fountain. Giant cookie in one hand, sandwich, peppermint pinwheel, and Coke in the other, Eleanor sat down and smiled into the children's faces. Some of them smiled back at her. As their glee spread contagiously to Eleanor's spirit, and the water spray arched above their bouncy little bodies, the joy of Jesus never felt more Real.

Though Eleanor's eyes most likely proved to be a bit bigger than her stomach, she returned to the conference nourished in body and soul—wrapped in a blanket of laughter, renewed with happy smiles. Ready for the next session on—yes—eating disorders.

Picnics on the Grass

As Eleanor recounted her story to me just before the afternoon lecture began, a smile of satisfaction crossed her face, and I wished I'd been along for the delightful break. I'd have traded in an instant the roundtable professionals' discussion, served up with a roast beef plate lunch, for the simple joy she'd encountered as she witnessed the passionate play of the children.

Spiritual Passion

YOU SHONE YOUR SELF UPON ME TO DRIVE AWAY MY BLINDNESS. YOU BREATHED YOUR FRAGRANCE UPON ME . . . AND IN ASTONISHMENT I DREW IN MY BREATH . . . NOW I PANT FOR YOU! I TASTED YOU, AND NOW I HUNGER AND THIRST FOR YOU. YOU TOUCHED ME—AND I BURN TO LIVE WITHIN YOUR PEACE.[3]

ST. AUGUSTINE

There's something very passionate about spirituality. A quality that woos us, invites us to enter in deeper, makes us want to experience God with all our senses. As women, our quest for God arises out of a sense of incompleteness. An untamed inner need reaches out, groping for fulfillment that will only be satisfied with the Divine. We long for wholeness and union with God. The more we have of Him, the more we want of Him, and the more aware we become that we cannot live without Him. After all, God created us for His pleasure, glory, and companionship.

I've heard some people compare spiritual passion to physical intimacy, but perhaps most women are more likely to align spiritual fervor with childlikeness. That sense of delight in the present moment—tasting a new flavor of ice cream for the first time, smelling a bubbling pot of wassail at Christmas, hearing your favorite kind of music, touching the soft skin of a newborn baby.

We passionately experience the presence of Jesus in everyday life by being *aware* He is with us. Remember? He said He'd never, ever leave us. We are His beloved. As we rediscover childlikeness, reclaiming parts of our souls that we once discarded because we thought they weren't acceptable, passion is rekindled in our spiritual lives. When I started making space in my day for what I call "rocking chair time," a time to just sit and let myself feel loved by God, I found I wanted more and more of Him. In her poem *Love's Eternal Wonder*, Amy Carmichael aptly expresses a hunger for God, and a deep knowing of His loving presence we all long for:

> LORD BELOVED, I WOULD PONDER
> BREADTH AND LENGTH AND DEPTH AND HEIGHT
> OF THY LOVE'S ETERNAL WONDER,
> ALL EMBRACING, INFINITE.
>
> NEVER, NEVER HAVE I BROUGHT THEE
> GOLD AND FRANKINCENSE AND MYRRH,
> IN THE HANDS THAT GROPING, SOUGHT THEE,
> PRECIOUS TREASURES NEVER WERE.
>
> WHAT WAS THAT TO THEE? THE MEASURE
> OF THY LOVE WAS CALVARY.
> STOOPING LOW, LOVE FOUND A TREASURE
> IN THE LEAST OF THINGS THAT BE.
>
> O THE PASSION OF THY LOVING,
> O THE FLAME OF THY DESIRE!
> MELT MY HEART WITH THY GREAT LOVING,
> SET ME ALL AGLOW, AFIRE.[4]

Sacred Communion

WE WAKE, IF EVER WE WAKE AT ALL, TO MYSTERY.[5]

ANNIE DILLARD

It was Passover week. Each year I fantasize about having enough time to drive to one of the larger churches in Dallas to attend daily liturgical services just before Easter. Although I belong to a Protestant church, something about the more liturgical ceremonies calls me to enter in more deeply to the sadness and joy of Maundy Thursday, Good Friday, and Easter Sunday. This year I again thought of the sacredness of the Lenten season, but before I knew it, I'd neglected canceling commitments, my time was booked up, and I hadn't cleared the calender. But Saturday night, the evening before Easter, was open.

In a moment of serendipity, I asked Frank to join me for a private Easter Eve celebration of holy communion in our own living room. He accepted my invitation. After finishing our dinner that Saturday evening, Frank busied himself with chores while I got things ready: a cracker to symbolize the body of Christ and two cups of grape juice to commemorate His shed blood—nothing out of the ordinary. I spread out an old wool afghan on our hardwood floor and placed the cracker and juice beside a red dinner candle. Then, as an added personal touch, I filled a slender glass bud vase with cool water and added a single long-stemmed red rose.

Frank came into the living room just as I was adding the rose to our ceremonial spread of elements. As he dimmed the lights, I put on some appropriate background music. *It's a good thing to share sacred moments,* I consoled myself when an awkward sense of embarrassment and self-consciousness threatened to steal the joy of the moment.

Holding out his arms, Frank began with a blessing: "Come, Lord Jesus, we invite You to a celebration in Your honor. Come and be with us in any way You choose." Those words would grow in significance as the evening wore on. . . .

As the music played softly, Frank motioned me over to sit beside him in our swivel rockers. But first, I withdrew the rose from the vase, stood, tore the petals from the base of the stem, and sprinkled them over the afghan on the floor, symbolizing, to me, drops of Jesus' sacrificial blood. Then, handing the crackers and juice to Frank, I set my goblet on the blue velvet footstool. As I sat down, my goblet fell over and the grape juice spilled.

Somehow, mysteriously, the sacredness of that moment overtook the urgency of clean-up. I wish I could adequately describe the spilling of the grape juice. As the goblet fell over, the juice literally leaped into the air. Waves of purple, cresting into rivulets, then transforming into another shape, seemed near-suspended in mid-air. Almost as if in slow motion, the drops began hitting the carpet. The next instant, a mass of purple liquid lay in a glimmering pool at our feet. Splattered purple grape juice. Spilled blood of our Savior. Life-giving sacrifice for our sin.

Red. Shimmering. Liquid. I could almost hear the cry of Jesus, "My God, My God, Why have You forsaken Me?"

The beauty of that moment is beyond my finite description. It was as if God suspended time and held back thoughts of trivial concerns so that we could enter into a unique kind of communion with Him. Frank and I stared at each other in unbelief. After a few seconds, we recovered, panicked over the mess, and cleaned up. But for that one sacred moment—which I wouldn't have missed for all the spotless carpets in the world—we were with Jesus in a way of His choosing. We offered our presence to Him, and He came to us in an unexpected way.

In *Life of the Beloved*, Henri Nouwen tells the following story to illustrate the beauty of the brokenness of humanity put under the blessing of belonging to God. I believe it also demonstrates the mystery of God coming to us spontaneously, in unexpected ways—His ways—to surprise us with His joy and presence.

"Toward the end of Leonard Bernstein's *Mass* (a musical work written in memory of John F. Kennedy) the priest, richly dressed in splendid liturgical vestments, is lifted up by his people. He towers high above the adoring crowd, carrying in his hands a glass chalice. Suddenly, the human pyramid collapses, and the priest comes tumbling down. His vestments are ripped off, and his glass chalice falls to the ground and is shattered. As he walks slowly through the debris of his former glory—barefoot, wearing only blue jeans and a T-shirt—children's voices are heard singing, 'Laude, laude, laude'—'Praise, praise, praise,' Suddenly the priest notices the broken chalice. He looks at it for a long time and then, haltingly, he says, 'I never realized that broken glass could shine so brightly.'"[6]

This story reminds me that God comes to us moment by moment, in ways we cannot really predict. Sometimes in the glimmer of broken glass, and at other times in the beauty of spilled grape juice. He invites us to take rides in the wheelbarrow with Him, and to picnic on the grass. He delights in our availability and our grateful hearts. To Him, such things are far more significant than utilitarian results. And as we spend long days with Him in the garden, enjoying His presence, little by little, we're growing more Real.

Fake Fur
Perception:

The Christian life should consist only of productive activities, service,
and good works. Enjoying the pleasure of God's company
is hedonistic and self-indulgent. We enjoy God
only by reading His Word.

Real Skin
Reality:

A vital part of walking with God and loving Him is enjoying the
pleasure of His company. Loving Him with my heart and soul, as well
as with my mind, is not a waste of time, even if there is no utilitarian
outcome for the time spent.

*A*nd so time went on, and the little Rabbit was very happy, so happy that he never noticed how his beautiful velveteen fur was getting shabbier . . . and all the pink rubbed off his nose.

CHAPTER 12

And So Time Went On . . .

One of the few, yet rarely discovered certainties of life is this: if we are sensitive and open to God's presence we find all of life becoming more sacred. As the days pass, our concept of God grows larger and we begin to recognize the love of Jesus coming to us in the twinkling eyes of a little old lady. The joy of God in a child's face. The agony of Christ in a young mother's tears as she mourns the death of her newborn son. In spite of getting pink fur rubbed from our noses by life, we gradually realize that God has always been in control, always aware, ever present with us, even when we didn't feel Him near. Over time, we see that even when life does not turn out the way we envisioned it would, God never stopped loving us—not even for one moment. The kiss of God's presence is always there. Our part is simply to abide, to stay with, to live *in Him.* To become more Real.

———————

Bang!

At the sound of gunshot, I look out the window, startled. My grown sons are out behind our house on the "back forty." Brent's beautiful chocolate Labrador retriever, Boomer, is in training session—sitting by her master's side awaiting command.

"Break!" yells Brent, and off goes Boomer, streaking through the ankle-high grass in pursuit of the decoy. She loses the trail and looks back toward Brent. He motions to the left. Boomer follows his direction and retrieves the decoy. Heading back toward Brent, eyes fixed on him, Boomer begins to smile. (Dogs CAN smile, you know. You can see it in their eyes.) Without ever breaking their visual bond, the loyal dog returns to her master's side. "Good girl," Brent soothes, as he strokes her coat. "That's my girl. Good girl," he repeats. Boomer literally radiates joy as Brent continues to lavish her with his approval—the only reward she seeks.

Seeking God's approval above the often hollow praise of others is one way we can cultivate intimacy with God. He wants us to keep our eyes on Him day by day, follow His direction, and pay attention when He tells us we're off track. Like Boomer, we deeply need to see our Master's approving eyes and hear His assuring Voice saying, "That's My girl. I love you."

Soul Cafe

The church Frank and I now attend is quite small. There's a warm, family feel when we gather together, and I secretly (perhaps selfishly) hope we never grow so large that we lose this sense of connectedness to one other. On Saturday nights the youth open the church doors to the community and offer fellowship and a place to just hang out, play games, and shoot the breeze. They call it the *Soul Cafe*, based on the book with the same title (by Leonard Sweet). An array of food, fun, and fellowship is offered to anyone who will just show up.

Have you found a *Soul Cafe*? A place to just hang out, connect with someone, find some nourishment for your soul? The church seems to be succeeding at teaching the written Word of God these days. For that reason, I haven't said much about it in this book. That base has already been covered. Perhaps what we're not doing as well in the church is creating a safe place for being Real as we discuss tending the soul. Finding a fellowship of accepting believers can help us see God more clearly in the everyday moments of life.

The spiritual journey is a unique quest for each person. Just as God deals with us personally, we owe a certain reverence and respect to each other's individuality. Finding a non-threatening community setting where we can freely discuss the variety of ways the Holy Spirit feeds our souls can help us connect with others and encourage spiritual depth and exploration. And people are looking for the nourishing reassurance of acceptance and love. (That they are worthy and capable of connecting with God and other people.) I see this more and more in my work as a therapist. Many people are suffering from poorly nourished souls. When we isolate ourselves from God and others, instead of interacting freely with Him and His people, we often turn to compulsive habits and a myriad of addictive behavioral patterns that only lead to the roadblocks and rabbit trails we've already discussed.

And So Time Went On . . .

I feel very fortunate to have found a church where an atmosphere of openness and honesty prevails. Our pastor leads the way by vulnerably sharing his own experiences with prayer, soul-searching, and Bible reading. He hastens to add that the way he practices spiritual disciplines are not the "right" way for everyone, encouraging each of us to seek God individually, wholeheartedly. If you don't have a *Soul Cafe* atmosphere in your church, perhaps you can look for a small group where people share honestly about spiritual life. Or if you can't find such a group, be daring. Consider starting one.

Sue Monk Kidd addresses our need for tending the soul in her book, *When The Heart Waits.* "How little attention we Christians have paid to the soul as the seed bed of divine life within us. We've mostly looked at it as something to SAVE—an immortal essence in need of redeeming. How many souls have you won? This becomes the central question of Christian life. But the soul is more than something to win or save. It's the seat and repository of the inner Divine."[1] Like the miracle of childbirth, salvation of the soul is a life-giving beginning. Once born, a baby girl will learn to walk, and skip, and run, and turn somersaults, even dance in the wind. While birth began her life, *growth* enriched it.

We have become so fearful of New Age influence that I'm afraid we are neglecting the Ancient Age of the psalmist and others who practiced meditation, heartfelt prayer, and soul-searching. "As the deer pants for streams of water, so my soul pants for You, O God," said the passionate psalmist.[2] In the thirst of a forest creature, David recognized his own longing for His Maker. "Where can I go from your Spirit? Where can I flee from your presence?"[3] he asked, fully aware of God's ever-present love. "Search me, O God, and know my heart; test me and know my anxious thoughts,"[4] cried the soul-searching shepherd boy, inviting God to examine his wide-open heart.

Where is our spiritual passion these days? Why aren't we talking about God as if He's a vital, living part of our existence as David did?

The aim of honest conversation about caring for our souls is not to compare ourselves with others or rate our spiritual lives, but to stop compartmentalizing spiritual life. To cease thinking that worship is just for Sunday morning and prayers are for bedtime. To begin to welcome God into all of our moments, and to see threads of His presence artistically woven into the fabric of everyday experiences. Just as we sometimes share hot dogs with friends on paper plates, and at other times we serve up helpings of juicy pork tenderloin on our best china, there are a variety of ways to offer hospitality to God. Sharing with others the ways we are finding to live close to God is soul nurturing and helps us develop deeper interpersonal relationships with others.

The Velveteen Woman

IT IS OUR SOUL THAT GUIDES US TO BECOME REAL, AND THAT YEARNS FOR GOD AND HIS REALITY AND WAY OF PERSISTENT INTEGRITY.[5]

J. KEITH MILLER

Still Points

Are there places where you feel especially close to God? Perhaps the mountains remind you of God's majesty. Or walking along your favorite beach convinces you of His timeless love as the waves lap against your weary ankles. I call these deep places where we feel in touch with God our *still points*. It's good to be aware of settings that bring you to a quiet sense of contentment with the Lord, where you're not especially asking God to *do* anything. Instead you become intensely aware of what He's already doing. Still points are places that help us become more aware of God in everyday life. They allow us to wrap our hearts in a blanket of renewal and provide a kind of spiritual retreat from the noise of the world.

Sometimes we need to spend a larger-than-average chunk of time away from the telephone and other distractions to listen with open hearts to God. Life can get awfully chaotic and, if we are aware of it, we may sense our souls straining for a renewing rest, a season to relax, to let down pretense, and to embrace ourselves just as we are today. Paradoxically, when we take the time to examine our own lives in the shadow of God's abiding presence, we are free to forget ourselves and turn our focus onto Jesus and other people. I once thought it was not a good thing to become self-aware—that one needed only to be *God-*

aware. I have since learned that the two go together. And making time for still point connections with God is one way to grow more like Jesus, more Real.

VERY EARLY IN THE MORNING, WHILE IT WAS STILL DARK,
JESUS GOT UP, LEFT THE HOUSE AND WENT OFF TO A SOLITARY PLACE, WHERE HE PRAYED.

MARK 1:35

And So Time Went On . . .

On a beautiful day in late March, when the mercury rose to a long-awaited seventy degrees, Frank went on an afternoon-long spiritual mini-retreat. He didn't have to go far—just down to the creek, about five hundred yards behind our house.

"Do you love me?" I heard my husband's full, rich tenor voice echo through the woods singing the refrain of Tevye's question from *Fiddler on the Roof.* The previous evening, we'd been to see a high school rendition of the play with some friends whose kids were performing. Frank often breaks out in song while working, so I wasn't sure whether he was directing the musical question to me in playful expectation of a response, or whether he was deeply engrossed in a spiritual moment. I decided to risk it.

"Do I *what?*" I called out from the deck in a loud, off-key bellow, mimicking the voice of Tevye's wife, Golde. Suddenly the cows beside the creek took off running, and I spotted Frank, perched in a tree above them, laughing. He didn't answer, so I assumed I had distracted him. Later that evening, Frank told me he'd actually been calling out to God, asking Him for some assurance in the midst of a relational struggle with his son. The creek side is one of Frank's still points. Somehow, climbing up into a tree, with nothing except the sounds of nature to distract him increases Frank's awareness of his own heart cry for God's company.

Have you discovered some *still points?* Are there places where you go to let yourself sink down deep into God's presence without distraction? Henri Nouwen says "You must believe in the *yes* that comes back when you ask, 'Do you love me?' You must choose this yes even when you do not experience it. Return to it after every failure."[6] Can you do this? When you picture God's face, can you see Him smiling at you?

The
Velveteen
Woman   *Couch Time*

Any good marriage counselor will tell you that if you want intimacy in your marriage, you'll have to invest some time cultivating a relationship. In working with married couples, I often suggest they spend ten minutes a day sharing genuine affirmations and listening accurately to each other. I call this "couch time"—a few minutes each day devoted to a kind of vulnerable sharing that helps husbands and wives connect.

"Ten minutes? That's all?" a typical couple might say, insisting that it won't be enough time. But after trying the "couch time" exercise for a few weeks, couples often discover it's difficult to find even a few minutes together with no distractions. "The kids had their activities. We were tired. We were busy this week," they say. Regardless of the reason, there seems to be a definite correlation between the *quality* of their relationship and time spent together focusing on each other without distractions.

As in marriage, if we want a quality relationship with God, we need to spend some "couch time" each day cultivating it. We need an everyday way of meeting with God. It's not really the place that's important. For me, it's a rocking chair. For you, it may be a couch, a porch swing, or the kitchen table. The important thing is that we set aside quality time to commune with God regularly. Time to ask God to search our hearts, to see His smile, feel His comfort, know His approval. "To pray is to listen to the Voice that calls you the Beloved."[7] Setting aside time in our busy lives to listen to God as if He's really there—this is the important thing. The issue becomes not only, "Do you *believe* in Jesus?" but "Are you *connected* to Him?" Is the relationship Real for you?

Do you know how to just sit still and let God love you? How does that happen for you? Saint Teresa of Avila said that difficulty in one's prayer life comes from one fatal flaw, and that is praying as if God were absent. How often I have mindlessly rattled off my list of requests, never pausing to hear a reply, as if I were really sitting there all alone.

As if He were absent. If we have such difficulty with the "couch time" exercise, focusing attention on our spouse for just ten minutes daily, it makes sense that we may have to practice being present with God, finding aspects of sacredness in everyday moments.

And So Time Went On . . .

Just showing up each morning to sit in my rocking chair and meet with Him becomes a simple act of love. It may be an inspirational and dynamic time one day, and the next day I might nod off. I must resist the temptation to rate the quality of my time with God by measuring how it makes me feel. Emotions are a beautiful part of our humanity, but they lead us on an endless roller coaster of ups and downs. The point is to come to our meeting place day after day and offer ourselves to our Master.

As I look back on my days of living with God, I now see that my prayer life was once a sort of "Quick Stop" for the soul. A place to run into and get a cool drink and a full tank of gas all in five minutes. I did all the talking, usually asking for a bunch of blessings. If I asked on behalf of others, I considered myself unselfish, virtuous, methodically checking off concerns as I went down the list. Prayer was a thing to be answered. I'd rate my prayer life by how many requests got answered. I earned bonus points if they were answered the way I *wanted* them to be answered. I had no idea of how to take time for *listening* to God. Perhaps some of you have also settled for one-way walkie-talkie messages instead of a quality relationship. For long distance conversations—hollering at someone way over on the other side of the valley—instead of having an intimate chat with someone whose home is in your heart.

Although I certainly don't have prayer figured out, I do know that when I put away my checklist and sat in silence, prayer became a space of uncluttered rest. A two-way conversation. A time to listen carefully and to be heard. Perhaps listening to God's words in Psalm 139, and then personalizing them to myself, causes me to come away from prayer time with a hint of sacredness lingering, hovering over my day. Even though I may not understand God's ways of answering prayer, I can become content with the simple gift of His presence in my life, day after day.

I've learned that prayer is not a magic wand to wave about so I can get what *I* want. It's opening my heart to Him in surrender, so He can get what *He* wants. If you thrive on list making, try writing down things you are grateful for, as well as your prayer requests. Then spend some time listening to the silence, giving His Word and His presence a chance to speak to you. Let Him remind you of things to be grateful for.

Open yourself up to creative possibilities in your prayer life as well as your private worship and Bible study times.

Please don't get me wrong. I'm not saying you shouldn't pray for others, or for your own needs. God loves to hear our requests. My cousin Ham shows up at church each Sunday morning with pockets full of candy. He loves it when children come and talk to him, and after their brief conversations he withdraws a sweet treat from his pocket. The kids keep coming back Sunday after Sunday, and my cousin the "Candy Man" revels in the company of the little people.

In a similar way, God loves for us to come to Him and make our requests. He enjoys our coming back again and again, day after day, to ask for His favor. But if we are to become transformed to Real, we'll have to pull up a chair and visit, linger awhile, and get to know Him personally, not just learn *about* Him. It's difficult to get to know God intimately if all we ever do is hold out our hands asking for candy. "We are so caught up in what is urgent that we have overlooked what is essential."[8] God created us to have relationship with Him. As in marriages and good friendships, genuine relational closeness doesn't just develop accidentally. It takes time, focused attention, and patience.

Head Knowledge or Heart Knowledge

Perhaps I misinterpreted the church's message, but for a lot of years, I thought learning Bible facts was all it took to gain a rich, spiritual life. Of course, a clear understanding of the Scriptures is crucial to Christian maturity. The Bible is not only inspired, it's relevant. A solid grounding in the Scriptures is imperative to intimacy with God, and attending or teaching a Bible study can go a long way in training us to accurately interpret God's written message. But too often we read it to dissect it or to analyze it instead of discovering truth about God and ourselves.

I don't know about you, but I discovered my heart was simply not satisfied with accurate, scientific deductions. I could outline and chart a chapter of Romans and still miss God. Truth that has the power to transform a life has to penetrate deep into your soul and move from your head to your heart. It must become more than a theological certainty. Tony Campolo said in a recent public address, "I need to *feel* God, not just an argument from the intelligencia. I need an explosion of the Holy Spirit in the depths of my being."[9] That's a brave and vulnerable statement in the evangelical world. I believe we need to keep this perspective to attain a balance of truth and personal encounter with God, which is often neglected in our churches today.

Wounded Christian

When I asked one woman what denomination she belonged to she replied, "I don't really know anymore. Wounded Christian, I guess."
Wounded Christian.

There are lots of those around today. Accepting the frailties in the church has been an area of struggle for me. Many of my clients have suffered terrible emotional wounds at the hands of their Christian brothers and sisters. Sadly, in churches as in families, we are often hurt most by those who claim to love us. Something in me wants Christians to be above reproach. I find myself easily forgiving a murderer, or extending grace to a drug addict. But it's amazingly difficult for me to forgive hypocrisy within the church. Because of my own woundedness in this area, and the hurts of those I work with, it's hard to overlook the church's emphasis on doling out facts, when most women I talk to are very well aware of God's laws and justice. But they have never really come in touch with His love.

Yet, with all her frailties, the church is the Bride of Christ. And God forgives us for being human. "He knows our frame and remembers we are but dust."[10] I'm finding that as I become more aware of my own sinfulness, and more secure in God's love and acceptance, I'm more able to extend grace to others within the church. We are all really just beggars, sinners, and hypocrites, whether we realize it or not, and the best we can do is share with others in our circle of friends where we are finding some spiritual food. How we are discovering truth. Ways we are connecting with God. That's what church is really about—being family. Learning and growing together, being imperfect together, forgiving one another, loving one another. Because Jesus loved us first.

The Ebb and Flow of Life

"And so time went on . . . " says the story of the Velveteen Rabbit. And so, it's true for us, too. Over years and decades, with the ebb and

flow of life, we come to God and go back into the world, we get hurt and we do some healing, we win and sometimes we lose.

Because God Himself is a vast ocean of love and mystery, we can't predict unexpected ways His spirit might bless us with a moment of inspiration. We never know when He may surprise us with a joyous touch of His glorious presence. Such a moment came to me this past year at—of all places—a speaker's conference.

I'd learned a lot at Carol Kent's *Speak Up With Confidence* seminar and tonight was the closing session. Don and Anne Denmark had flown in to join Carol and members of her family for the final sessions of the conference at a church in Dallas. The finale would be a dramatization by the Denmark Duo. As I recall, the silent, two-person role-play was intended to demonstrate the power of nonverbal communication. Expecting to learn more about the mechanics of public speaking, I was not prepared for what would follow.

After a brief introduction, Don and Anne began. A large lilac shawl was their single prop, and not a word was spoken. Anne skipped toward Don, then stopped, blushed, and turned away briefly. Then she looked back at him again. Both were shy at what appeared to be their first meeting. Smiling, Anne looked into Don's face. He smiled back and reached for her hand. Then, together, they faced the audience and held up their arms as if offering thanks to God.

Next, Anne spread the shawl onto the floor picnic style and sat down. Don joined her. As the couple gazed into each other's eyes, turning their heads first this way, then that, you could almost make out a conversation. *Tell me about your family. How many children do you want to have when you get married? Will you marry me?* They held hands again and this time they kissed—just a slight, brief brush of their faces. Then the couple stood, faced the audience, and lifted their arms to God, again, in thanksgiving.

It wasn't hard to guess what was happening in the following scenario. When Anne covered her head with the shawl, those of us who were sitting in the audience knew they were portraying—you guessed it—a marriage ceremony. As the couple stood together, Don pushed back the veil-like shawl, and kissed his bride. Then they turned to face the audience and an imaginary voice in my head said, *Ladies and gentlemen, may I present Mr. and Mrs. Don Denmark.* Then the couple lifted their arms heavenward. *Thank You, Lord Jesus, for our marriage.*

Then, Anne rolled up the shawl and held it in her arms, the way

The Velveteen Woman

a woman would cradle a baby. As she rocked her imaginary newborn, Don walked up behind her, rested his hand on her shoulder, and together they admired the first addition to their family. Then Don and Anne each placed one hand on the baby bundle and raised their free arms into the air. *Thank You Lord, for blessing us with a child.*

The next scenario was a bit more nebulous. Anne's facial expression changed markedly, revealing fear, even panic. She paced the floor as Don looked on, then picked up speed as if running to peer out the window to check on a teenager who'd stayed out past curfew. Twisting and wringing the shawl and turning toward Don, she held her hand to her mouth, anxiously biting her nails. Then Anne took a few steps toward her husband. He embraced her, offering comfort. Then, facing the audience, they put one arm around each other and raised their free arms into the air as if voicing a heart cry. *Lord, we don't understand Your ways. Please take care of our kids.*

Anne then wrapped the shawl around her waist and tied it in the back, apron-style. She walked slower now, and her back was slightly bent. Don walked slower too. They appeared to be washing and drying the dishes together. Then, turning toward each other, they smiled, embraced, faced the audience, and held their arms up to God. *Thank You for long years of life.*

Then, with backs even more bent, Don limped over to Anne. With great affection, she touched the side of his face, leaned forward to kiss his cheek. As she did, Anne held her back, as if in pain. Together, slowly, the couple turned toward the audience and raised their arms to God. *Lord, thank You for my beloved companion in old age.*

In the last scenario of the dramatization, Anne is even more unsure of her steps. She labors to drag a kitchen chair to the middle of the floor. Don is trying to walk to the chair. He stops. Pain streaks across his face. He grabs his chest, and Anne helps him, slowly lowering his body into the chair. He slumps over. Anne touches Don's face, as if to whisper his name. He does not respond. Anne weeps. Then, slowly, reluctantly, she wipes her face with her apron. Untying it from her waist, Anne wraps it lovingly around her beloved's shoulders, stroking his hair, his face, as she cries. But he is still. Anne pulls the shawl up over his head, covering his cold, lifeless face.

Anne strokes Don's shawl-covered head and shoulders. Then she bends slowly down to hold her face close to his one last time. She lingers there as if savoring this moment. Then, Anne pushes herself to her feet and labors to straighten her time-worn back as much as she can. Alone now, she stands. Slowly—ever so slowly—she raises both arms to God.

It's just You and me now, Lord. I'm so glad I have You.

Although this simple, silent role-play certainly succeeded in demonstrating the power of nonverbal communication, it also brought me up short, on a much deeper level, piercing my heart with full force. Here was a couple going through their days, returning to God after each life event, through its ups and downs, day after day. Whether sick or well, young or old, they returned to God over and over. Whether they understood His ways or not, whether they were happy or sad, fearful or brave, together or alone, they simply and humbly returned to God.

Ah, this is how God transforms us into Real as we abide in Him, I reflected, wiping a tear from my cheek as the dramatization concluded.

Day by day, little by little.

As the Skin Horse said, becoming Real happens "bit by bit."

WHAT MAKES AUTHENTIC DISCIPLES IS NOT VISIONS, ECSTASIES, BIBLICAL MASTERY OF CHAPTER AND VERSE, OR SPECTACULAR SUCCESS IN THE MINISTRY, BUT A CAPACITY FOR FAITHFULNESS.[11]

BRENNAN MANNING

Fake Fur
Perception:

There are certain appropriate times to be spiritual,
such as at church, when studying the Bible, or doing good deeds.
Other mundane life experiences have nothing to do with God.

Real Skin
Reality:

As I abide in Christ, all of life becomes more sacred,
and I become more Real.

PART 4

Let's Get Real

He didn't mind how he looked to other people, because the nursery magic had made him Real, and when you are Real, shabbiness doesn't matter . . . you can't be ugly, except to people who don't understand.

CHAPTER 13

Shabbiness Doesn't Matter

"Gimme my Blue Bear! He's mine!" four-year-old Scott exclaimed. While my young son didn't mind sharing his Leggos, Fisher Price Play Barn, or Star Wars figures with his younger brother, his favorite stuffed toy was off limits. "I want my Blue Bear!" Scott demanded again, just before giant tears formed in his eyes. Brent refused to surrender Scott's most treasured possession, and it was time for Mom to step in.

Over the years, Blue Bear could be seen in our family photos as Scott's faithful companion. Eventually, he lost a button eye and began to take on a different color from so many hugs and kisses—a nondescript color, actually closer to brown than blue. Still, we always referred to this toy, with affection, as Blue Bear.

My son loved Blue Bear because it was *his* bear. The jelly stain by the bear's ear reminded Scott of Pastor Hobson's Passover breakfast, when he'd accidentally spilled strawberry preserves on the stuffed cub. The oil stain on the back of Blue Bear's head instantly recalled fun memories of the day Scott helped Dad change the oil and spark plugs in the car. Blue Bear's stains and smudges didn't make him ugly to my young son. They were marks of fond experiences that only proved Scott's relationship to his favorite little companion.

Just as Blue Bear's shabbiness confirmed his place as Scott's favorite toy, and just as the Velveteen Rabbit's shabbiness did not make him ugly to the Boy who loved him, we are not undesirable or unlovable to God just because our lives are marked with imperfection. God loves us, scars and all, because we are *His*.

What is *shabbiness*? I think of it as the flawed thread of imperfection that connects us to other human beings. We balk at admitting it, especially as grown-ups, but it's a part of us all. Shabbiness is not having our act all together, and feeling okay about it. Being Real in the midst of our shabbiness is being childlike and transparent, able to enjoy a healthy laugh at ourselves. Letting our smudges and stains show because they are evidence of the life experiences we've shared with our Master. Most of all, it's finding our purpose in belonging to Him.

Being Real means embracing the gift of self-acceptance, instead of pretending to be perfect. Just BEING—shabby spots and all. As we become more relaxed with our faults, all the energy we once put into looking strong, defending our reputation, and being "together" is freed up for authentic living. Then, the joys of childlikeness—transparency, curiosity, fascination with simple things—float to the surface of our Real skin selves. And as they do, don't be surprised if silly giggles and laughter begin to bubble up in the process.

Childlike Vulnerability

THE KINGDOM BELONGS TO PEOPLE WHO AREN'T TRYING
TO LOOK GOOD OR IMPRESS ANYBODY, EVEN THEMSELVES.[1]

BRENNAN MANNING

It's a mistaken notion that we must abandon the child within to become mature. Eric Berne, founding father of a psychological theory called Transactional Analysis, emphasized how necessary it is to play, to be amused with life's little pleasures, to enjoy the present moment as we grow up. To be childlike lifelong. He insisted that although we can overdo playfulness and need to strive for balance and appropriateness, an open-eyed childlike attitude is necessary and fundamental to sound mental health. Like Berne, I have observed that most people who experience psychological distress lack any semblance of playfulness. On the other hand, those who seem to find the silver lining of every storm cloud are most often a bit lighthearted and carefree.

When I think of all the qualities that endear my closest friends to me, childlike vulnerability is near the top of the list. One friend in particular comes to mind, one who lives in a near-constant state of childlike playfulness. Becky enjoys a responsible career as an author, speaker, and columnist, while squeezing the joy out of life, one moment at a time. Our frequent lunch dates sometimes resemble a tea party for ten year olds, and occasionally turn into heart-to-heart talks sprinkled with our little-girl tears. But one thing always stays the same—Becky will be Becky, shabby spots and all. There will be very little pretending or hiding from her feelings. Like the Velveteen Rabbit, she's not too concerned about how she looks to other people. Whether Becky is conversing with a famous talk-show host or the best buddy of her eleven-year-old son, she is equally likely to let fly with a side-splitting episode of the continuing saga of her lost car keys. She's the most "untogether" person I've ever known and, truth be told, that's why I love her so much. Becky helps me feel comfortable with my own shabbiness. She makes me want to be warm, real, and relaxed—like her. Not only does Becky have a knack for laughing at her own mistakes, she's also willing to nondefensively share them with others.

Shabbiness Doesn't Matter

"You'll never believe what happened to us on the way home from your house last night," Becky's perky voice spoke from the other end of my phone receiver. Six close friends from our small, newly formed church had gathered in our home for dinner and conversation, and Becky had left feeling encouraged.

"See, Scott?" she said to her husband as they drove home. "Did you notice how Coyle complimented my work as an author? That's the kind of encouragement I want you to give me." (Although Becky and I had exchanged horror stories about our furtive attempts to spur our men on to being better husbands by pointing out "examples" we'd like them to follow, only to find we'd bruised their egos instead, she must have had a brief memory lapse.)

"Boy, was that ever the *wrong* thing to say!" Becky exclaimed. "Scott pulled the van over to the side of the road, handed me the keys, and said he needed to walk. I thought sure he'd change his mind and come back to the van, so I just sat there and waited. And waited. And waited."

Becky continued her tale. For a brief moment, I held my breath, still a bit unsure this story about a couple I dearly love (they're two precious gems on opposite ends of just about every spectrum) was headed toward a happy ending. The tone of her voice quickly set my worrying mind at ease. So I pulled up a kitchen chair and refilled my coffee cup as I listened to Becky explain what happened next.

The Velveteen Woman

It seemed that when Scott did not return to the car, Becky got in the driver's seat herself, started up the engine, and began combing the streets of Farmersville to find her man. By this time, any anger she may have harbored had turned to sheer panic. Here she was out on a country road at nearly midnight, alone, and for all she knew, her husband might have been captured by the local skin heads she'd just passed in the town square.

As it turned out, when Becky turned the car around, the headlights shone out into a cornfield and there in the middle of the field was—you guessed it—her husband, Scott.

"I yelled at him to get back in the car but he said 'no way,' and just kept on going." Becky said. Just then, she noticed a set of bright headlights approaching. *Oh no, not the police!* she thought, cringing. Swallowing her fear and pasting on a confident smile, Becky rolled down the window and started trying to explain how they, a couple who'd been married over twenty years, were just having another of their newlywed spats.

"At first, the policeman didn't believe me," Becky said. "But when Scott saw what was happening, he came running to my rescue yelling, "Officer, it's true. This is nothing serious, just a lover's quarrel." In a split second, it was apparent Scott wasn't about to abandon his lady in a moment of real need, in spite of his hurt feelings. Becky summed up her story by saying that when the policeman found out she was Becky Freeman, author of a book called *Marriage 9-1-1* and writer of a monthly magazine column by the same title, he ended up confiding some of his own marital problems. So, making the best of the situation, Scott and Becky offered an on-the-spot counseling session on the value of staying together, even if you need to take a walk to cool off once in a while! *Marriage 9-1-1* in action.

Perhaps she and the policeman made a pact to never again compare their spouses with other men and women, I'm not sure. But Becky and Scott did drive away without a citation for violating curfew, and by the time her story came to an end I was laughing uncontrollably. Here was my dear friend, showing her own marital shabbiness to a police-man at midnight, and then telling me all about it the next day without apology. Why, I'm quite sure if that had been me (being a recovering perfectionist and all), I would have guarded that story with my life!

Becky and I share a small circle of close friends, and one of them said to me recently, "She never gives you the impression she's perfect, so there's no need to feel intimi-dated." On other occasions, Becky has shared many other equally revealing stories. Using lighthearted humor as a connecting link to other women, Becky finds many ways to say, "Hey, I'm imperfect, and it's okay if you are too." Even her book titles reflect warmth and human-ness. *Worms in My Tea* gives you the feeling right away that no matter how hard one tries, there's always a fly in the ointment somewhere, but it's okay. *Marriage 9-1-1* blinks the message: even in a stable marriage, there are times when emergency sirens go off. It's no wonder that every-where Becky goes, women cluster around her, eager to talk, hoping some of her humor, optimism, and realness will rub off on them.

If sharing ways we are shabby *connects* us with others, makes us feel closer, then what holds us back from sharing more vulnerably? From the conversations I've had with women, two things seem to keep us from being transparent: insecurity and shame. To be sure, some life experiences are so wounding they cannot be laughed off. Even if they could, it wouldn't be appropriate to share them in just any group. But many times, as grown-ups, we are ashamed of just being imperfect, causing ourselves a lot of misery when a lighter approach would serve us much better.

And then there's the matter of insecurity. Ah, yes, that one gets all of us sooner or later. I think even someone as childlike and vulnerable as Becky would have to admit there are times when she hides weakness or pretends just a bit when she's feeling insecure. Nobody's perfect—not even at being shabby. Insecurity is the part about being "grown up" that's different from when we were children. Years of living in a fallen world teach us to protect ourselves, and we become unsure it's okay to relax with our faults.

Lee Ezell, author of *Will the Real Me Please Stand Up!* reinforces the idea that we connect with others when we talk about our shabbiness. She says "speaking of our strengths separates us from one another; speaking of our weaknesses unites us."[2] See-Through Christian is the term Lee gives to those who live transparently, letting Jesus show through. To be transparent means:

> *to open our hearts.*
> *to be frank.*
> *to exhibit guilelessness.*
> *to be easily detected or seen through, to be obvious.*
> *to be readily understood and clear.*
> *to be honest, unpretentious, and approachable.* ³

THE STRONG ARE NOT ALWAYS VIGOROUS, THE WISE NOT ALWAYS
READY, THE BRAVE NOT ALWAYS COURAGEOUS, AND THE
JOYOUS NOT ALWAYS HAPPY.⁴

CHARLES SPURGEON

———————————

Just as living transparently—letting others see our faults—helps people feel more comfortable, boasting in our strengths and accomplishments tends to build a wall. I wonder if any of you have ever been intimidated by holiday family newsletters. I call them "brag sheets," and I confess, I just hate to see them coming. Last Christmas, however, an exceptional letter appeared in the stack of holiday mail. It was from some old friends, a family of five, and their vulnerable letter turned out to be a treasured holiday gift. A "see-through" surprise, all wrapped up in beautifully transparent paper.

After a brief opening, Mark and Lana (not their real names) began a story that took three pages to tell. It seems that Lana had a baby out of wedlock at an early age and put the baby up for adoption. All this happened before she met Mark. As the years passed, Mark and Lana had three children, two boys and a girl, and now there were grandchildren. Lana bared her heart, sharing with intimate friends in this newsletter that not a single day had passed when she did not think of the baby she gave away, a baby girl, whom she had never known. The children were never told about the birth of the "out of wedlock" child, though Lana did tell Mark before their marriage, unwilling to have a secret between them.

The purpose of Mark and Lana's newsletter was to share the joyous news that the long lost daughter had somehow "found" her birth parents, and that they'd already had one reunion. Family members were adjusting to the surprising news, but they were so happy to have things out in the open. How refreshing! Vulnerability. Joyous shabbiness. Holiday warmth radiated from this family's openness. So different from the typical list of accomplishments that so often left us feeling separated from others. Instead, Mark and Lana's letter *connected* us to them because they found a way to send the message: Our family is not perfect, and it's okay if yours isn't either.

Shabbiness Doesn't Matter

THERE IS NO HOPE FOR ANY OF US UNTIL WE CONFESS
OUR HELPLESSNESS. THEN WE ARE IN A POSITION TO RECEIVE GRACE
. . .SO LONG AS WE SEE OURSELVES AS COMPETENT
WE DO NOT QUALIFY.[5]

ELISABETH ELLIOT

―――⋅∗⋅――⋅∗⋅――

Let Jesus Shine Through the Cracks

Shouldn't we try to be a good representative for Jesus? Yes. Of course, we should. But I think sometimes we get the wrong idea about how this is done. We don't impress others when we put up a front or act stronger than we really are. In fact, Jesus shows up best in our weaknesses. This idea was beautifully reinforced for me recently on a Sunday morning.

Pastor Coyle had just finished his sermon and opened a discussion.

"Now let's hear from some of you," he began, inviting comments from the congregation. During the few seconds of silence, I thought of a brief conversation I'd overheard between Coyle and another man he was encouraging just minutes earlier during the morning coffee break. "Our son has had some problems too," Coyle had said compassionately. "I think I can identify with your struggle." Now, here was a man demonstrating a different kind of vulnerability. Not necessarily child-like, or humorous, but definitely transparent and connecting. Refreshing. Inviting others to be equally open, our pastor continued his invitation. "I don't have all the answers," he said, "so let's just learn from each other. Who has something to say?" (Did you ever notice how the people who know the most about things don't need to boast? Coyle is well versed in the Bible, ministry, and life experiences, yet he chooses to remain teachable, even by those much younger and less experienced than he.)

The Velveteen Woman

"I have a question," a high school-aged girl opened the discussion. "I want so much to be a good witness at work," she stated sincerely, "but I mess up so often." Close to tears, the young girl said, "I mean, I try hard, but I always blow my testimony by losing my temper, or laughing at a dirty joke, or something like that." After a moment of silence, a man I'll call Don spoke up.

"You know, I once thought my 'mess-ups' made God look bad," Don said. "It grieved me deeply, because I messed up often. But one day, near Christmas, a young associate at work gave me a note," Don went on. "I was shocked and amazed to read that the young man saw Christ in me!" After a brief pause, he continued, "I think our lives are sort of like broken clay pots, all cracked and chipped in spots. But somehow, the light of Jesus shines through the cracks."

"Yeah," agreed another man in the congregation. "Me too. God has a way of making Himself known to others, through our shabby lives."

"Just be honest about being a broken vessel," Don encouraged the young girl who had vulnerably shared her heart's concern. "Don't worry about trying to be a witness. You can't make others see God in you. As weird as it sounds, if we just show our human weakness, it encourages others that they could be a Christian too." Then Don summed up, "God is faithful to shine through the broken cracks."

RELIGION IS FOR PEOPLE WHO ARE AFRAID OF GOING TO HELL.
SPIRITUALITY IS FOR THOSE WHO HAVE BEEN THERE.[6]

ROSE V.
MEMBER OF AA

Becoming Real means accepting our weaknesses and being vulnerable. Letting others see Jesus through the cracks in us. Becky connects with others using a lighthearted kind of humor and childlike openness. Pastor Coyle opens others up by sharing his own imperfection and identifying with others' struggles. I sometimes think the rest of us would do well to follow the example of AA groups in being completely vulnerable with others from the get-go: "Hi. I'm Brenda W. and I'm a sinner." Perhaps that would help remind us again and again that we're on the same level at the foot of the cross, sinners in need of God's grace.

Have you been hiding your stains of insecurity and trying to fill in the cracks with your own abilities? Are you afraid your shabby imperfections will make you ugly to God? Jesus is the only person who ever became totally *Shabbiness Doesn't Matter*

Real, yet had no spiritual shabbiness—no sins on His record. However, because of God's unconditional love for all of us sinners, Jesus *became shabby*, took on our sin so that we could be brought near to God. "But now in Christ Jesus you who were once far away have been brought near through the blood of Christ."[7]

Even though we've been brought near, many of us are not experiencing nearness, intimacy with Christ. I believe we can. As we gain courage to let more of our Real skin show, we discover ourselves loved by God, shabby spots and all. It occurs little by little, as we enjoy the present moment and get more comfortable with our oil spots and jelly stains. When we are able to admit, "Hey, I don't have all the answers."

Then, as childlike curiosity reawakens, we are free to ask questions. Lots of questions . . .

Fake Fur
Perception:

If I let others see my faults and struggles, they won't like me.
They'll think I'm incapable and incompetent if I don't have my act
together. God expects me to be perfect too.

Real Skin
Reality:

Revealing our weaknesses helps others feel connected to us.
Fully understanding and unconditionally loving us shabby
humans, Jesus shows up best in our weakness. He shines brightly
through the cracks in our flawed armor.

What is Real? Does it mean having things that buzz inside you and a stick-out handle? Does it hurt? Does it happen all at once . . . ? Or bit by bit?

CHAPTER 14

Real Questions

Marget recalls saying prayers with her mother and two sisters when she was a little girl. One night they knelt by the bed in their pajamas with eyes closed and hands folded. "Now I lay me down to sleep, I pray the Lord my soul to keep. If I should die before I wake . . . If I should die? IF I SHOULD DIE?" Suddenly little Marget was on her feet, eyes wide open. "Mommy! I don't want to die! Why am I *saying* that?"

I wonder how Marget's mom would have answered this question. She was a thinker, even as a three or four year old. But today, Marget doesn't recall an answer. She only remembers that she asked a pressing question about something she'd been absentmindedly reciting over and over. When we're young, we seem to know intuitively that it's okay to ask questions when curiosity strikes. It's a natural, healthy part of life.

Recently I was talking with my good friend Linda on the phone. "How are the girls?" I inquired about her two toddler daughters.

"Oh, just fine," Linda responded, chuckling. "Naomi continues to challenge me with her daily round of questions. Brenda, she's either really intelligent or totally out in left field." Linda went on to explain. "The other day Naomi asked if ants have chins. I don't know where all these deep thoughts come from!" my friend concluded. We laughed together as our conversation wound to an end. Preschoolers often test their parents' patience with an endless chain of "whys" and "why nots."

"Do restaurant potties flush by their self?" I recently overheard the high-pitched voice of a pint-sized person in one of the stalls in the ladies' room at the pancake house.

"No," responded her mommy. "Only airport potties flush by themselves."

"How 'bout boat potties? Do they flush by their self?" the toddler persisted.

"No. Now hurry up, our pancakes are getting cold." Who among us has not come to the end of our wits at the hands of a curious toddler? Isn't it interesting how many of us gradually lost our sense of wonder and anticipation as we moved through our middle school years? At some point, it became more difficult to ask questions. By the time we reached junior high, our teachers had to prod and coax: "The only stupid question is the unasked question." Still, we were reluctant, unsure of ourselves, fearful of rejection from young peers. Sadly, as we grow up, we lose the spontaneous freedom that prompted the Velveteen Rabbit as he quizzed the Skin Horse: "What is Real?" "Does it hurt?" "Does it happen all at once?"

Sometimes, without ever meaning to, adults may send children an unspoken message: "Don't ask. It's too much trouble. Too upsetting." We could just admit we don't know if ants have chins or whether boat potties flush by themselves. (At least I don't know, do you?) We could simply observe, "My, you're really curious today." But as parents, we are often preoccupied, or haven't yet learned to be transparent with kids.

Unfortunately, many churches also unintentionally discourage exploration and stifle spiritual curiosity, quickly giving black-and-white answers as soon as questions are voiced. The unspoken message: "Don't think, don't doubt, don't question." Sometimes the instant answers hurled at us don't ring true. Charles, my counseling mentor, said many times that identifying questions is more important than finding answers. That fulfillment comes as we learn to trust that answers will emerge gradually. His wise words brought to mind a quote I had run across from the poet Rilke:

"Be patient toward all that is unsolved in your heart. . . . Try to love the questions themselves like locked rooms and like books that are written in a very foreign tongue. Do not now seek the answers, which cannot be given you because you would not be able to live them. And the point is, to live everything. Live the questions now. Perhaps you will then gradually, without noticing it, live along some distant day into the answer."[1]

In our culture, we're conditioned to *answer* questions, not to embrace them or let them linger to be turned over again and again in our minds. "There's an art to living your questions. You peel them. You listen to them. You let them spawn new questions. You hold the unknowing inside. You linger with it instead of rushing into half-baked answers."[2] No matter what our age, whether we are a child whose parents are getting a divorce, an adolescent wondering about the ramifications of having an abortion, a man who just lost his job—we need to identify our questions and *live them*, instead of suppressing them.

Real Questions

Naming Our Questions

Occasionally, I have the opportunity to help a child voice his or her important questions to parents. I must say, helping little people learn to communicate is one of my favorite tasks as a therapist.

"You want to hear about an amazing concept, Miss Brenda?" twelve-year-old Martin asked during his fourth session.

"Sure," I replied. It wouldn't be the first profound idea to come from this kid. Martin's mother brought him in for therapy because his grades were dropping, his teacher said he was becoming withdrawn, and he had lost several pounds. A storehouse of creative ideas and scientific genius, young Martin proceeded to explain to me how starfish reproduce. He hoped to become an oceanographer someday.

"Now, Martin," I said, redirecting our conversation, "we're going to have a meeting with your mom tonight. I want you to think about what you need to ask her. Some of the questions you've brought up to me, perhaps?"

"Okay," replied my young, logical-minded client.

"Tonight's your chance. Ask away," I coaxed. "Your mom may or may not have the answers you want, but it will help you feel better if you ask the questions on your mind." Martin's parents had divorced during the previous year, and Dad had given Mom a year to come back home if she wanted to consider remarriage. But for her own reasons, Martin's mom had taken up with a young boyfriend and was not about to let him go. And Martin had something to say about that.

"Mom, how come you didn't come back home?" Martin asked, as his mother squirmed in her chair.

"Martin, you won't understand this," she replied curtly, "but I am with Bob now, and he needs me."

"But I need you too, Mom," Martin asserted. "Why is Bob more important to you than I am? Don't you love me?"

"Of course I love you," Martin's mom started in, shifting her weight uneasily as she offered the most convincing reasons she could muster to explain her departure and restate her plans to stay with her boyfriend.

"Okay, but I still want you to come back," Martin bravely concluded. I ended the session and thanked Martin's mom for her willingness to face her son's questions. Although he didn't get the answers he hoped for, the air cleared a bit between the two of them, and Martin got some of the heaviness out of his chest. A bit of relief. It helped.

Wrestling with Our Questions

Although we seem to be driven to discover answers, a lot of healing actually occurs when we identify our questions and begin to honestly grapple with them as Martin did. Even though this truth has been demonstrated to me over and over by clients and friends, I'm afraid I still find myself easily drawn to the role of problem solver. When clients lay their questions at my feet, looking expectantly into my eyes, I am acutely aware of the temptation to give them simple, pat answers. Answers I know are inadequate for life's hardest questions. Statements that sound right and proper, making me look and feel important. Like a toddler's mother, sometimes I want to give "yes" and "no" answers. But I've found this isn't usually what people really need.

Once clients have identified their important questions, therapy is off and running. Then it won't be long before they "graduate"—set themselves free to explore life with a rediscovered sense of curiosity, sort of like they had as little girls. Now that they are women, instead of asking whether ants have chins and restaurant potties flush by themselves, their "grown up" question are more open-ended: "Who am I?" "How can I learn to trust?" "Why am I afraid to love?" "Why am I afraid to ask?"

Sometime after my faith crisis I finally settled into an acceptance of questions. I mentally tucked them into my knapsack and wandered along a bit more happily. I'd name some of my questions and, now and then, take them out and wrestle with them, do a little pondering and musing. Pretending to have all the answers instead of recognizing important questions can be very costly. Having learned this lesson the hard way as my first marriage ended, I hope to pass on the value of freely examining life and relationships as we walk down the path toward Real.

YOU CAME HOME LATE AND DIDN'T CALL,
YOU TIPTOED QUIETLY DOWN THE HALL.
YOU DIDN'T TELL ME WHERE YOU'D BEEN.
. . . I DIDN'T ASK.

YOU READ THE PAPER AND THE MAIL,
I ASKED YOU HOW YOUR DAY HAD BEEN,
YOU TOLD ME, "FINE," AND THEN WITHDREW.
. . . WE DIDN'T TALK.

THE FEAR THAT HELD MY QUESTIONS BACK
IS GONE NOW, AND I'M NOT SURE WHY.
I HAVE A LOT TO SAY TO YOU
. . . BUT NOW YOU ARE GONE.

Julie sat down at my kitchen table for a no-nonsense conversation. My neighbor from a few houses down our country road was looking for some direction and a place to rest. Tired of merely breathing, going through the motions of being alive, Julie was desperate for a change. At midlife, she no longer wanted to play the good girl if it meant remaining emotionally dead. I applauded her desire to break out of a false mold of pretense, but I was also concerned. In this heady-with-freedom state, women like Julie often end up in the Hot Zone. The pendulum can easily swing from "I'm a good girl!" to "Look out world, I'm ready to be bad!" as if there were no midpoint. Like many women at this stage of life, my neighbor was not only exploring new ways of thinking and feeling, she was toying with the possibility of having an affair.

After a cup or two of coffee, it was plain to see that I was not about to talk Julie out of the course she seemed determined to pursue. Then an idea popped into my head. *A few poignant scenes from a good movie might help her more than mere words from me,* I mused. I suggested Julie rent *The Age of Innocence,* thinking perhaps she might identify with Countess Ellen Olenska. The countess was a beautiful and vulnerable woman with courage enough to question high society's "hieroglyphic world where the real thing is never said or done or even thought." In the movie, the countess stands in sharp contrast to her cousin May Welland, who spends her time planning social affairs, smiling sweetly, doing just what is expected. May is too fearful to ask any questions, and it would eventually cost her plenty. Newland Archer is a wealthy attorney engaged to the lovely, but shallow, May. When the complacent Newland meets Ellen, he is thrown into turmoil, helplessly drawn to her unconventional charm.

When I'd first seen the film a few years before, several scenes crystallized in my mind, demonstrating how wrestling with our questions helps us become more Real. One such scene occurs when Ellen laments, "The real loneliness is living among all these kind people who only ask me to pretend." Then come the questions, "Does no one cry here?" "Does no one here want to know the truth?" "Are women here so blessed they never feel need?" Questions I think many of us need to ask in our churches. As the plot progresses, Ellen falls passionately in love with Newland. However, as she wrestles internally with her complicated feelings, she decides an affair would require deception. Ellen is committed to being a genuine woman. Yes, she loves Newland, but he had promised himself to May. A commitment to genuineness would not allow her to take what could not be completely hers.

During another pivotal scene, the countess gazes wantonly into Newland Archer's eyes. Slowly, she takes a few steps away from him as if to gather her thoughts, then asks, *"Is there anywhere we can be happy behind the backs of those who trust us?"*

It was a brutally honest question, one addressed as much to herself as it was to Newland, and one that demanded a choice be made. This was the question I hoped would capture Julie's attention. I'd seen so many lives swept away, destroyed by the currents of passion only to find—too late—that they were drowning in a river of betrayal and pain. *If only people would ask this question of themselves sooner, rather than later,* I'd thought. *Perhaps Julie will ask this question to herself,* I silently hoped.

Julie had a lot to talk about when she came to my house again, a few days later. She began by saying she'd watched *The Age of Innocence,* and enjoyed the visual Victorian feast of fancy satin and velvet party dresses and elegant table settings. Then she admitted how strongly she related to Ellen Olenska's struggle. Here at my kitchen table, she felt safe enough to talk about her own real-life attraction to an emotionally responsive man who was not her husband.

"Mike is my supervisor at work," Julie asserted, reluctantly. "Being around him has become the highlight of my life—an emotional fix."

"What is it about Mike that makes you feel so special?" I asked.

"Oh, simple things. Maybe he'll say, 'You're really an asset to the company,' or he'll ask me about my kids. But the warmth of his smile makes me feel like a teenager again." Julie responded, glowing.

"So, he's meeting emotional needs for you."

"Oh yes! I think he's the only person who even *tries* to understand me. I sense a flow of energy with him—it seems to come with the mingling of our chemistries." Julie explained that things weren't going well at home. Her husband's business was failing, and he was preoccupied. The kids had left home. She was desperately trying to find a life.

What do I do when I feel things I *shouldn't?*" Julie asked, frustrated. "How close am I to acting on these feelings? I'm committed to my marriage and to God, but how can I just keep plodding along with life as it is?"

"Good questions," I acknowledged. "You know, Julie, sometimes our souls, if left unattended, can become emaciated, wanton. A sexual experience can look like the quickest, easiest fix—a shot of heroin for the passion starved. What are your questions and feelings trying to tell you about yourself? What's missing in your life?"

Responding to Julie with my own set of questions, I affirmed her for facing up to temptation. Like the countess, she was unwilling to deny her honest thoughts and feelings. As Christians, we often fail to recognize the importance of self-awareness. But if we are to "take captive every thought to make it obedient to Christ"[3] we must first *recognize it,* and *then bring it under control*—not push our thoughts away unaware, denying the temptation. It is often our awareness of thoughts that dispels their power over us. That day, Julie realized a choice had to be made, or she'd be swept away with her feelings.

During the following weeks, Julie reconnected with God by acknowledging her temptation. She began to discover new ways to nurture her soul: a hidden passion for acting. A natural talent for making flower arrangements with her home-grown roses. Julie learned to channel her God-given passions into wholesome areas that would enhance her marriage instead of destroy it. The hot winds that blew through Julie's midlife years finally calmed into warm currents of gentle aliveness—the kind of energizing Julie had really been looking for all along.

And it all began with questions. A few intense, heart-searching questions.

Perhaps at some time, you have opted to be like May Welland in *The Age of Innocence,* afraid to ask too many questions because it's just easier to pretend. Have you been afraid to face temptation? Unaware that asking questions might be very helpful, even necessary? To remain like May is to grow numb, frozen in fear, never becoming Real. Denying and pretending feels safe because we don't have to risk. But playing it safe has a high price tag. It costs us our Real selves.

Have you ever noticed that Jesus did not shy away from questions? They were often His way of confronting, teaching, or providing a thought-provoking answer. "Who do you say that I am?" "What are you looking for?" "Do you want to get well?" "Why do you not understand what I say?" Jesus took many risks and refused to pretend. As the supreme example of what it means to be Real, it comforts me to read of this Man of many questions. Like Him, we sometimes feel alone—isolated—with honest questions as our best companions.

AN ANSWER BEFORE AN HONEST QUESTION
DOES DAMAGE TO THE SOUL.[4]

HENRI NOUWEN

One day as we munched on chicken salads at Applebee's, my friend Karen asked, "What's wrong with me? I go to the ladies' Bible study every week, and I'm the only one who seems to have any problems." She went on to explain her confusion. Karen had asked others in the group to pray for her brother, who was struggling desperately to earn enough money to support his family. "I'm so concerned about him," she said, with a furrowed brow. "And when I tell the other women, they stare blankly at me. I want to ask them how we can sit there week after week talking about the Bible as if it doesn't even relate to life. As if it were just a storybook. I want to ask them, 'Don't you have any problems? Do you ever cry? How is it that your life is so together?'"

"Why don't you ask them these questions," I challenged, in between bites. But for the time being, Karen decided to remain quietly complacent in the group and put her fake fur "mask" back on. The church she attended seemed unanimous in their resolve to maintain a conspiracy of silence. The unwritten creed was the same as the one parents of curious toddlers often adopt: "Don't ask. It's just too much trouble." In such a restrictive environment, one word of truth can sound like a pistol shot. And Karen wasn't ready to be identified as the shootist.

Instead, after the ladies' meeting was over each week, she went home from the group meeting feeling alone, sometimes crying by herself, feeling guilty for having more questions than answers.

Karen began to journal her feelings, honestly expressing her loneliness, confusion, and desire to connect with the other ladies in the group. With her permission, I gratefully share the following lines from her journal:

My heart breaks. We are the church and we stay inside the doors, shutting out the hurting instead of reaching out a helping hand. Is this how the love of God works?

My heart breaks. I feel so alone and I wonder what's wrong with me. Am I the only one with these concerns?

My heart breaks when words are used only to express facts, and when dreams are too silly to repeat. When sounds and smells and sights don't provoke memories or imagination. When the soft hair on a dog's nose isn't comforting. And when the first day of fall doesn't make a heart skip a beat.

You'd say, "What trivial concerns! We have more serious matters to think about." And I'd say you're right. But when I look at you, I see the eyes of those who have forgotten how to look at life with wonder and joy. I see loneliness and emptiness and drudgery.

Look into my eyes. Is that joy hiding? Or was it ever there? Can a mind learn to accept things as they really are after learning what they should be?

My heart breaks. What a blessing to be Don Quixote and to battle windmills instead of giants . . . and not know the difference.[5]

Although Karen held back her questions for a short while, she was too Real to pretend very long. Unable to find safety for sharing her honest feelings in church proved frustrating. Soon, however, she and her husband were asked to lead a worship group. Within a few months this group grew into a small congregation—a new church was born. As you can imagine, one of their goals in this endeavor was to provide a relaxed setting where people can be more vulnerable, where questions are valued, and fear of rejection is not such a threat.

HOW LONG WILL THE ENEMY MOCK YOU, O GOD? WILL THE FOE
REVILE YOUR NAME FOREVER? WHY DO YOU HOLD BACK YOUR HAND,
YOUR RIGHT HAND?

PSALM 74:10-11A

God never intended us to stifle our relevant questions. He's not
the least bit intimidated by them or threatened by them. Nor is He com-
pelled to give us answers. After all, He is God. Near the end of the book
of Job, when God answers Job's questions from out of a storm, He doesn't
give many answers, really. Instead, He asks His own questions to put
things into perspective.

"Where were you when I laid the earth's foundation? . . .
Who marked off its dimensions? . . .
Who stretched a measuring line across it?
On what were its footings set, or who laid its cornerstone —
while the morning stars sang together and all the angels shouted for joy?"[6]

Just as God's query reminds us of His sovereignty, we need to
remember that while it's healthy to ask questions, we may not get many
answers. God's thoughts are not our thoughts, His ways are not our
ways. As time passes, we learn to ask our questions and let go, to
believe even when our questions are unanswered, and to live worshipfully within the mysteries that lie beyond God's revealed purposes.

Embracing Our Questions

THERE ARE YEARS THAT ASK QUESTIONS,
AND YEARS THAT ANSWER THEM.[7]

ZORA NEALE HURSTON

If we want things fixed, nailed down, and all figured out, living
with questions will be miserable. Family therapist Virginia Satir so aptly
stated, "Most people prefer the certainty of misery to the misery of
uncertainty."[8] But if we can get comfortable not having the answers
today, and get on with embracing the questions themselves, we can
begin to relax and live in freedom.

As you may recall, my search for a love that was powerful enough to transform life began with the question *"What is Real?"* Asking that question opened the door, and relationships with friends became more transparent. A few seemed to hold little substance and fell by the wayside. I began to feel more alive.

The questions I once held back: "Do You love me?" "Why couldn't my marriage be saved?" "How can You forgive me when I've made so many mistakes?" were

now being recognized, explored, occasionally pondered, and deeply valued. But they weren't always answered. As this realization began to creep into awareness, my once black-and-white life took on hues of Technicolor, one after another. I began to relax. Questions could be asked, but they no longer drove me crazy. When I asked, *How long, O Lord, must I bear this burden?* He might respond: *Long enough.*

Oh. Okay.

At last I began to recognize God's sovereignty as the most adequate of all answers. His presence as my main source of security. When I was a little girl about six or seven, I used to sit beside my dad in his rocking chair while he watched television. Dad was hard of hearing, so the volume was usually turned way up, and he often watched sports or political reviews, and I wasn't really interested in the programs. I just loved sitting beside my dad in his favorite chair. Sometimes I would rest my head on his chest, and I could hear the slow, steady beating of his heart as he breathed in and out. It was as if nothing in the world could harm me as I sat in the security of my dad's presence, snuggling close to his heart.

I think perhaps this is how it is with God. We learn to relax by His side even as we hold our unanswered questions. Knowing that He knows the answer is enough. This is a part of the mystery of life with God. It's *His presence*—sitting close to His heart—that brings security, not knowing every answer to life's unending questions. Like a child resting her head on her mother's breast, we learn to rest contentedly on our Master's chest.

AND SHALL I PRAY THEE CHANGE THY WILL, MY FATHER,
UNTIL IT BE ACCORDING UNTO MINE?
BUT, NO, LORD, NO, THAT NEVER SHALL BE, RATHER
I PRAY THEE BLEND MY HUMAN WILL WITH THINE.

I PRAY THEE HUSH THE HURRYING, EAGER LONGING,
I PRAY THEE SOOTHE THE PANGS OF KEEN DESIRE;

SEE IN MY QUIET PLACES WISHES THRONGING,
FORBID THEM, LORD, PURGE, THOUGH IT BE WITH FIRE.

AND WORK IN ME TO WILL AND DO THY PLEASURE,
LET ALL WITHIN ME, PEACEFUL, RECONCILED,
TARRY CONTENT MY WELLBELOVED'S LEISURE,
AT LAST, AT LAST, EVEN AS A WEANED CHILD.[9]

AMY CARMICHAEL

The Velveteen Woman

Fake Fur
Perception:

To trust God and have faith in Him means I should never
ask questions. If I do question God, His Word, or pat theological
answers, He becomes angry.

Real Skin
Reality:

Asking questions is a part of the intimate relationship
God wants to have with us. However, He may not give us many
answers. Gradually, we become comfortable asking questions, and
more content resting in His sovereignty.

Nearby he could see the thicket of raspberry canes . . . in whose shadow he had played with the Boy on bygone mornings. He thought of those long sunlit hours in the garden—how happy they were—and a great sadness came over him . . . Of what use was it to be loved and lose one's beauty and become Real if it all ended like this? And a tear, a real tear, trickled down his little shabby velvet nose and fell to the ground.

CHAPTER 15

Bygone Mornings

On a crisp day in late October, I strolled through the historic district of McKinney, a charming little town near our home in the country. Meandering in and out of the antique shops lining the town square, I was enjoying the golden glow of a late Indian summer afternoon. A shop window displaying a collection of small doll purses sewn with tiny glass beads caught my eye. As I entered the quaint shop, an elderly woman glanced up from her lap work.

"How ya doin' on this glorious afternoon?" she greeted me.

"Fine. I'm doing just fine," I replied. As I walked closer to the old lady, I could see that she was working on one of the doll purses, sewing minuscule purple and yellow beads onto satin, in straight little rows.

"Your eyes must have weathered the years better than mine," I casually commented. "I don't think I could see well enough to do such delicate handiwork at my age."

"At your age?" she asked, as I noted a hint of cynicism. "Why, you're just a spring chick. Actually, I'm legally blind."

"Really?" I asked, amazed.

"Oh, yes," she went on to explain. "I can only see outlines of light and dark. It's just that I've always loved making intricate things. I do it mostly by feel."

"By feel?"

"Uh-huh," she said slowly, fumbling for the scissors. "If Beethoven can compose a beautiful symphony by thinking it in his head, without hearing it, I figure I can make glass bead doll purses by feel."

"Wow," I said, admiring her exquisite creation almost as much as her wise perspective.

The Velveteen Woman

Just as the Velveteen Rabbit recalled bygone mornings when he played with the Boy in the raspberry canes, we can all remember days when we were younger, perhaps happier, before we became wounded. But the losses of life cannot be avoided. Whether we lose our eyesight, a marriage, financial security, health, or a family member, it hurts to lose. Sometimes we are able to compensate for the loss, like the lady in the antique store. At other times, we may become aware of something we gain as a result of loss, a benefit we now enjoy, even though we still suffer from the loss.

Frank had an experience of this kind when he encountered a bout of polio as a seven-year-old boy. The disease set in just as his dad began a new job as school band director. His mother's income as a nurse was needed to help support the family of five. Unable to walk, young Franky was taken from his home in Kansas City, Missouri to stay with friends of his parents—an older couple who offered to care for him on their farm in Iowa. Though "Uncle Edmund" and "Aunt Louise" were strangers for a short while, it wasn't long before Frank felt right at home on the Valentines' farm.

"You lost a whole year of life with your family," I recall saying to Frank the first time he told me about this life-altering year. "Didn't you miss your parents and your sisters?"

"Yes. I missed them very much," he went on to explain. "I cried myself to sleep a lot of nights in the beginning, and I didn't know if or when I'd ever walk again. It was pretty scary." As Frank paused, I had a quick mind-flash of him as a pudgy towhead, with his two sisters, Karen and Marget, doing the dishes together as young children. He'd told me of ways they mixed a little fun with work, as one child washed, one dried, and one read a book aloud to the others. For a whole year, he missed out on intimate times of work and play with his beloved family. "But it was there on the farm with Uncle Edmund that I fell in love with the country." Frank's words drew me back to the present moment. "I've often wondered how my life would have turned out if I'd never had polio, never lived with the Valentines."

Over the years, Frank told me stories of the kind outdoor man he came to know as Uncle Edmund, a man who played classical music on a small Victrola beside the couch where Frank spent his days. And then there were the wintry afternoons when Uncle Edmund would plop Franky into a sled, tuck him in amongst a pile of warm, snugly blankets for a hand-drawn, narrated tour of the farm. As the kind-hearted man walked along in the snow, Franky in tow, he pointed out the winter homes of muskrats, beavers, and other furry little critters.

Bygone Mornings

"You make it all sound pretty warm and cozy," I said, gaining my own appreciation for this man. Like a black night salted with stars, Uncle Edmund sprinkled young Frank's darkest year with sparkles of hope.

"Yeah," Frank replied slowly, with a reflective smile. "I almost didn't want to get well."

Embrace Your Loss

Although Frank lost a year of time with his own family, he gained an appreciation for the wonders of nature, and relationships that would change his life forever. While it's clear, in this case, that gain resulted from loss, we can't count on that always ringing true. Sometimes losses can be so devastating they chill us to our very core. Perhaps after the loss of a child or a lifelong companion, it's hard to believe we'll even survive. At such times, weighing loss in terms of gain resounds in our souls like hollow blasphemy.

What do we do with our most painful losses? Hide them? Pretend they aren't really happening? Blame others for them? I suppose we do all of these things at times. But if we hope to heal, Henri Nouwen suggests in his book *Life of the Beloved* two helpful ways to respond: befriending our loss, and then putting it under the blessing of belonging to God. To heal, he says, is not to push away or disclaim our failures, lost hopes, dreams, and disappointments. But to claim them and carry them to the cross. As we lay our losses before Jesus in prayer, crying out to Him in our agony, He gives us comfort and hope.[1]

It helps me to think of God's love as a large umbrella covering me as a violent storm rages all around. I reach out and claim my broken past, with all its patchy bald spots—painful relationships with relatives, loved ones who have died, a dear friend caught in an addiction. I mentally gather these symbols of brokenness and loss, and hold them in my arms as I stand under the large, sturdy umbrella.

If I try to hold onto them while standing in the storm unprotected, my mind is overtaken with defeating thoughts such as, *I always suspected I was a worthless woman, an incapable mother, and now I am sure of it, because look what's happening to me. God is punishing me. He's mad at me and now I've lost my child, my husband, my job . . .* But if I stay under the covering of God's blessing—under the umbrella of His love as I hold my losses in my arms—I no longer need to curse myself. Covered with the protection of God's love, I find strength to accept my armload of loss. "When we need guidance in our suffering, it is first of all a guidance that leads us closer to our pain and makes us aware that we do not have to avoid it, but can befriend it."[2]

Somehow, as we stand *with* our pain, we become stronger *through* it. Welcoming the darkness of loss teaches us that it is not something horrible to be avoided, but a place of new strength and unexpected gifts. I discovered this truth on a deeper level a few years ago, when I decided to embrace the loss of intact family by "reframing" our family portrait.

"I'm so excited!" squealed my friend Linda as she piled family photos of her husband and two daughters on the kitchen table until the wooden surface was nearly covered. "Isn't this a nifty way to create a special family album? Look at these neat scissors!" My friend held up three pair of small scissors that cut paper in zigzags, scallops, and squiggly patterns. An array of colored papers and stickers for making a creative photo album lay strewn on the floor beside the table.

"Wow," I managed to say, halfheartedly. For me, family albums were only reminders of brokenness and loss. I couldn't recall the last time I'd pasted pictures into a photo book, and I'd often caught myself wincing, quickly looking the other way when I came across such titles as *Let's Make A Memory* in bookstores. Ouch.

But as I drove home from Linda's house that day, my musing took a different direction. *Why shouldn't my children have a family memory book of their growing up years? Sure, our family had broken up. But my sons still had grandparents and family roots.* I turned the idea over and over in my head. With a bit of reluctance, I decided to try to "reframe" our family memories, to restore as much wholeness as possible to our fragmented family portrait, as well as acknowledge the reality of step-relationships.

I began by searching the malls in Dallas for some unique photo album covers. Something truly special. Different. Symbolizing the time-lessness of mother-son and father-son love. Just when I was about to give up on the seemingly endless shopping task, I came upon just the covers I'd been searching for. They were in the display window of the Bombay Company. Fine cher-rywood covers with brass name plates for engraving ini-tials. Yes. They had the look of a fine family heirloom. Perfect.

Then came the hard part. Sorting and selecting the pictures to be placed in the books. As I dug a mound of old family photos out of the bottom of the trunk, feelings I hadn't gone looking for began to stir. I only wanted to salvage a few family jewels from the wreckage of our history. But I found that even though ten years had passed since my divorce, I still winced a bit as I held the hard copy of our once happy family in my hands—pictures of Mom, Dad, and two sons all together. I guessed this to be the reason why I'd not often heard of people from broken homes making family albums.

Even so, as I shuffled through the stacks of old photos, my per-spective gradually shifted. *I can do this,* I encouraged myself. *I can do it for my sons. Which pictures illustrate similarity of father and son? Which ones will speak of love that will stretch over many years to come?* I wondered. *Perhaps this baseball shot of Brent as a seven year old alongside this picture of Dad as a volunteer elementary team coach? Yes. These shots show their mutual love of sports.* Working my way through illustrations of our years of liv-ing as a family, I finally came to the year of our divorce. *Should I stop here?* I questioned myself. *Why? Our lives continued on.* If I really wanted to align this pictorial remembrance of our lives as close to our reality as possible, I must continue.

Shuffling through the stacks once again, I added a recent shot of Dad and Stepmom laughing with two handsome college men. Mom and Stepdad and two guys with hunting dogs standing at their sides. Yes, this was our reality. Funny thing, it didn't hurt as much as I'd anticipated.

As it turned out, the project took me several months, so I decided to make Christmas gifts of the picture books. For my sons, these albums were the most treasured presents they would receive from me for a long, long time. Symbols of roots. Pictures of people—flawed people—who loved them. The wound of family brokenness would always be deep. The loss of an intact family a permanent scar. But eventually, the broken pieces were gathered and brought under the protection of God's love, and given as a gift.

SOMETHING MUST DRIVE US OUT OF THE NURSERY TO
THE WORLD OF OTHERS, AND THAT SOMETHING IS SUFFERING.[3]

C.S. "JACK" LEWIS

*The
Velveteen
Woman*

Recently I heard Dr. Archibald Hart, author and professor of psychology at Fuller Theological Seminary, speak at a conference in Dallas. Dr. Hart told of his own family's devastating loss when his son-in-law—a teacher, coach, and father of two young sons—was killed in a car accident. "I sat my two grandsons down at the breakfast table," Dr. Hart began his story, choking back tears, "I took a deep breath, and told them, 'your daddy died last night, and he won't be with us anymore.'"

"Papa, what do you mean?" asked the oldest grandson, as panic streaked across his face. "Why are you saying this?"

"I'm so sorry, boys," Dr. Hart sobbed, gathering his grandsons in his arms as they tried to absorb the devastating blow. "It's true. He's gone."

Then one night, Dr. Hart came home after a day of work at the seminary. Several months had passed since their son-in-law's death, and the family continued to mourn their loss. Following the faint sound of soft crying, Dr. Hart walked into the bedroom. There his wife, Kathleen, sat on the side of the bed, rocking herself as she cried, clutching a pencil sketch of Jesus holding a lamb in His arms. "Arch," said Kathleen. "Arch, can you just print some words across the bottom of this picture for me on your computer?"

"Sure, honey," Dr. Hart soothed his wife as he held her in his arms. "What words do you want me to print?"

Kathleen pulled away from her husband's embrace and held the picture out in front of her, staring at it. "Just print, 'hold me, Jesus.'"

Hold me, Jesus.

Do you ever need that kind of comfort? When life wounds us deeply, God's comfort is our only hope. Our disappointments and losses lead us into a natural process of mourning. Though we may try to tiptoe past it, fearing its flames may consume us, most of us won't find healing without walking barefoot through the coals of the grief process. Once we do, we find that though the coals are burning hot, Jesus walks with us, holds us, comforts us, and eventually gives us hope to go on.

Elizabeth Kubler-Ross has identified five stages that usually make up the process of grieving, though they don't always come in order, nor last the same length of time. Beginning with a shock response (denial), we move into anger, a time of bargaining, depression, and finally, acceptance. As we walk into the sadness of our loss, looking it in the eye while we sit securely in the lap of our Master, we begin to heal. I don't know about you, but I wouldn't want to try to face my life's most tragic moments without the comfort, protection, and love of God. I know I am not strong enough. But what I can do is claim my sorrows, gather them all up and, as Henri Nouwen says, "put them under the blessing." In God's strength, I can face another day, another month, another year.

Share Your Sorrow

> TO GRIEVE IS TO ALLOW OUR LOSSES TO TEAR
> APART FEELINGS OF SECURITY AND SAFETY AND LEAD US TO
> THE PAINFUL TRUTH OF OUR BROKENNESS.[4]
>
> HENRI NOUWEN

It was eleven-thirty at night when the phone rang. At least an hour past most people's customary cut-off point beyond which only urgent calls are made. Tragically, this was just such a call. An unfamiliar voice spoke on the other end of the line: "Please pray for Dennis and Jill. Scotty died tonight." I hung up the receiver, stunned. Frank and I had been out for dinner with friends and hadn't gone to bed yet.

"What's wrong?" Frank asked, placing his hands on my shoulders, looking directly into my eyes as I sat on the side of the bed, in shock. "What's happened?"

"Scotty Windsor is dead," I said in a monotone voice that reflected the numbness I felt inside.

After about thirty minutes of sitting with the unwelcome news, Frank and I knew we wouldn't be able to sleep, so we got into our car and drove to Dennis and Jill's. The ten mile drive seemed to last an entire day. As we approached the Windsor home, we saw a cluster of cars parked outside. It was the kind of middle-of-the-night gathering of friends and family that only happens when someone dies. As we got out of our car, we heard our dear friend Dennis crying—obviously overcome with grief. He appeared to be trying to explain something to a friend, pointing to his pick-up truck, which had rolled down the incline behind their house and hit a tree. Wally, a mutual friend, was walking down the driveway with his arm around Dennis.

When Dennis saw us, he opened his arms to embrace Frank. Tears fell freely as we all sobbed. "He's gone," Dennis wailed, gasping for breath. "Dear God, I can't believe it. My little buddy, my Scotty is gone . . . " More gut wrenching sobs followed.

As I entered the back door of the house, I noted the rooms were all filled with friends and family. Echoes of soft crying could be heard everywhere. Although it was way past bedtime, five-year-old Daniel was still bright-eyed, playing a card game with Wally's wife, Judy, on his bedroom floor. Catching a glimpse of me in the hallway, Daniel looked up, exclaimed, "I didn't know *you* were here!" and came running to give me a tight hug around the neck. "Why are you crying?" Daniel asked, unable to fathom the meaning of the cold, harsh word all the grown-ups were saying tonight: *death.* Unaware that his little brother—his Big-Wheeling buddy and daily companion—would not be back to sleep in the bottom bunk. Not tonight or any other night.

Just a few hours earlier, Daniel and Scotty had been playing in their backyard, dressed up and ready to go to an Octoberfest costume party at their church. Dennis had gone to a Promise Keepers gathering that Saturday and arrived home just in time to clean up for the party. Jill had been outside with the boys, and went inside for just a moment to gather some things for baby Jessica's diaper bag. In an instant, Daniel came into the house calling, "Mommy! Come Quick! Come now!"

As Daniel led Jill out into the yard, she probably expected to find (as mothers often do) that Scotty had skinned his knee as he fell from the swing, or some other typical childhood mishap. Instead, Scotty's little body lay on the ground. Somehow, mysteriously, the pick-up truck had rolled down the slope of their yard and crushed Scotty's tiny chest before hitting a tree. And five-year-old Daniel was the sole witness. Friends and family stayed through the night at the Windsor's home, huddled in groups of three or four, telling and retelling their interpretations of the horrible accident. Trying to make some sense of the fatal, final seconds of Scotty's life. Trying to grasp the reality of this young family's loss. Stunned by the shock of it. How did the pick-up truck begin rolling? How had Scotty gotten into the truck's path? There would be no answers for these questions. Not tonight.

It was around three in the morning before Frank and I headed back home, after several of us made plans to return after we tried to get a few hours of sleep. "We'll bring some donuts," we'd said just before leaving. Somehow it seemed there should be a way to offer some kind of real comfort, words that would truly console, something we could do or say. *Anything.* But there was no comfort. Only donuts.

Three days passed. Scotty's graveside service would be in the morning, with the memorial service following at three o'clock. As we drove up to the graveside, I gasped as my eyes fell on the tiny casket beside the mound of freshly piled dirt that would soon cover little Scotty's body. *Oh God, please don't let this be one of those "this should be a happy occasion" kind of services,* I silently pleaded. *I don't think I can handle that. And what kind of comfort would such hollow words offer to Dennis and Jill?*

As it turned out, the pastor shared a hopeful perspective without denying the gravity of the Windsors' loss. We listened to words from the Bible. We cried. We sang. Then we drove away from the graveside, numb. Frozen. In shock. A two-year-old child had died, and reality had not yet set in.

That afternoon at the memorial service, Jill, who usually took a backseat when it came to public affairs, courageously marched up to the front of the church to say a few words from her mother's heart. Her strength was almost eerie. (Have you ever noticed how God seems to provide some kind of "shock response" for the first hours and even days after news of a loss?) "I want to leave you with a few words about Scotty that only a mother can share," Jill began bravely. After telling her favorite memories of her daring, bouncy little tow-headed all-boy toddler, Jill quickly brought us all to tears with her final haunting words. They would echo in my mind for months to come: "We've lost our Scotty. I'm hurt, and I'm angry. I miss my son and I want him back. Please pray for our family." Clearly, Jill spoke of her own loss, and yet it almost felt as if it were mine. Her pain gently brushed across my heart and awakened sleeping memories, similar feelings. We shared unspeakable grief.

In the days and weeks that followed, Frank and I would watch our good friends struggle to live with the void Scotty left. To grapple with pain we'd never experienced. To go on living without their child.

Months passed.

One day, Jill shared her feelings with me over lunch.

"The books I have read mostly frustrated me," she confided.

"Especially right after Scotty's death. Nobody seemed to identify with my anger and loneliness."

"So, it might have helped if someone had put *those* feelings on paper? The anger and loneliness they experienced as they mourned *before* they came to resolution of their grief?" I asked, hoping to gain understanding.

"Yes, I think it might have helped," Jill explained. "Although I'm honestly not sure anything could have eased the pain. But that's when I felt most alone, most in need of someone to identify with, to connect with." Jill went on to say that she'd consoled herself by reasoning that the authors had written their books several years after their losses. Once they had regained some energy and strength. Jill admitted that although she'd tried, she had also been unable to vulnerably express her feelings in writing during the time of most intense pain. "I just survived," she said. "I think that's all you can do for a while. You survive."

After pausing to take a few bites of her baked potato, Jill continued, in a trancelike state. "I still have my days when I feel so lonely for Scotty, my arms just ache for him. Or sometimes I hear a sermon about heaven and it reminds me that my Scotty is there now too. It's just weird. It still doesn't seem right."

How do people recover from a grief as deep as the loss of a two-year-old child? Or do they ever? How does a person find hope in such a pile of devastation? Although each of us will experience different losses in life, sooner or later we all come to this point. It's when we say to God, *I didn't know things would end up like this! What am I supposed to do now, without my child? My financial security? My husband? My health?*

Of what use is it to become Real if it ends like this?

Scotty's Gifts

Just as the Velveteen Rabbit's sadness led the way to tears, so our grief eventually leads the way to healing. Like a little girl reluctantly exchanging an old, favorite jacket she has outgrown for a new one that fits her now-bigger body, we feel naked and chilled in the process of letting go of what has become familiar and comfortable for God's unknown blessing. But in time, our new coats of real skin are warmed and massaged with God's healing balm.

Dennis and Jill grieved with friends and family for many months. The day came when it was time to put Scotty's Big Wheel up in the attic and take his little clothes to the church rummage sale. The living room table which once displayed a large collection of photos of Scotty alone eventually held pictures of their other children, Daniel and Jessica, as well. But the memories of Scotty were ever present.

Then, one day there began to emerge from their ocean of loss, a glimmer of hope. The first warm currents of acceptance began to wash across their hearts. "As we feel the pain of our own losses, our grieving hearts open our inner eye to a world in which losses are suffered far beyond our own little world of family, friends, and colleagues . . . Then the pain of our crying hearts connects us with the moaning and groaning of a suffering humanity. Then our mourning becomes larger than ourselves."[5]

Out of the Windsor family's desire to carry on the memory of a child who is still very much alive in their hearts, Dennis and Jill began to pray to come in touch with families in need, who would be willing to receive help. It was their desire to give gifts to children in needy, hurting families during the Christmas season. Gifts they might have given to their own child had he lived.

"Scotty's Gifts" was born. It has now become a Christmas tradition in Dennis and Jill's hometown of McKinney, Texas. Each year before the holiday season, the Windsors send out a letter to many families explaining their tragedy. "Life is more difficult now, as we learn to live without our son," their newsletter explains. "Holidays prove to be the hardest times because we must spend them without Scotty. We feel the pain that other hurting people experience this time of year." Dennis and Jill traditionally collect gifts from generous families who are willing to share, and distribute the gifts to needy people in the area. As the project grew, a local church pitched in to help out.

The Windsors shared the agony of their loss with friends and family. Eventually, their pain led them into a cause larger than their own grief. No longer were the cries of the hungry and the lonely distant from their hearts and ears. Somehow, they found strength to reach out and hold hands with suffering humanity. Out of their own mourning, a song of gratitude was born. Gifts were given to the lonely and hurting, in the name of the child they had lost.

A Gift of Hope

And after a few more months passed, another gift was given.

Hope was literally born. Hope Elise Windsor. Born June 28, 1997. Oh my, what a joyful postscript she is to the Windsor's story. Inscribed at the bottom of the announcement of her birth were these words, lovingly scripted in her parents' hand:

> FOR I KNOW THE PLANS I HAVE FOR YOU,
> DECLARES THE LORD,
> PLANS TO PROSPER YOU AND NOT TO HARM YOU,
> PLANS TO GIVE YOU HOPE AND A FUTURE.
>
> JEREMIAH 29:11

Nobody would ever replace Scotty. But the memory of his life, and the hope of the future his family will one day share with him in heaven give the Windsors strength to go on. Not *only* to go on living, but also to reach out to others along the way.

As the Windsors touch the lives of hurting people with compassion, feeling their losses, they become increasingly aware of the ultimate loss of all time, God's loss of His own Son's life. Unfathomable pain. Intense cries of loneliness: "My God, my God, why have you forsaken me?"[6] Because of this supreme loss, we can become Real. In that day, we shall be like our Master—the One who has loved us for a long, long time. Not just to play with, but *really* loved us. Then, there will be no more tears. No more shattered family portraits. No more lost children.

Then we shall be completely Real.

> HE WILL WIPE EVERY TEAR FROM THEIR EYES. THERE
> WILL BE NO MORE DEATH OR MOURNING OR CRYING OR
> PAIN, FOR THE OLD ORDER OF THINGS HAS PASSED AWAY.
>
> REVELATION 21:4

*Fake Fur
Perception:*

Although some losses in life are unavoidable, there is no need to
grieve, because God is in control.

*Real Skin
Reality:*

Healing from loss only comes after grieving. As we bring our losses
under the umbrella of God's love, He give us comfort and hope.
Sharing our grief with others makes us more Real.

$\mathcal{I}$'ve brought you a new play fellow . . . $\mathcal{H}$e is going to live with you for ever and ever!" $\mathcal{H}$e was a $\mathcal{R}$eal $\mathcal{R}$abbit at last, at home with the other rabbits.

CHAPTER 16

At Last! At Last!

"I want to go home," Nell whispered. After a bout with infection, my "Texas Mother" entered the hospital and it appeared she might never leave. I was unsure of which "home" she was talking about. Well, okay. I knew she meant heaven—where she'd see Jesus face to face with skin on, and be completely Real—but I was reluctant to let her go. Sound a bit selfish? Yes, to be sure. As I spooned tiny bites of mashed potatoes and peaches into Nell's withered little mouth, I was not aware this would be the last time she'd eat solid food.

"Will you read to me from the book you're writing?" she asked, weakly.

"Sure. I'll read the chapter I wrote about you," I said. Thoughts of *The Velveteen Rabbit* came to mind as I read to her. Nell and I had often talked about the theme of the book I was writing—*The Velveteen Woman* —and discussed ways to weave women's life experiences into the story line. It occurred to me that Nell's reality was changing, just as the Velveteen Rabbit's reality had changed. With her fur completely rubbed off, Nell was lying in a little heap in a hospital bed, just waiting to step into heaven, just like the Velveteen Rabbit when he was waiting to become Real.

Although Nell had grown quite weak, I had to leave town the following day for a business conference in another state. When I returned, Nell was in intensive care. As I walked over to her bed, she opened her eyes and reached out for my hand. "It's your birthday today, you remember?" I asked. *Yes,* she nodded. The breathing tube the doctor had inserted to help with respiration made it impossible for her to talk. "You're seventy-four big ones!" I said, tying a ribbon to the foot of her bed. "They wouldn't let me bring in flowers, so I brought you

a balloon." Nell gave my hand a squeeze—a rare delight, because she usually avoided touching. It hurts too much when you have rheumatoid arthritis.

"You really are ready to go home, aren't you?" I asked, choking back tears. *Yes,* she nodded. *Oh, yes,* she said with her eyes as she shook her head up and down as vigorously as she could manage. *She must feel so vulnerable,* I thought to myself. *Already, I miss her outreaching love, her gentle laugh, and the humorous twist she added to life.* All of Nell's expressions of God's grace had been silenced. She'd lost everything except life itself.

I swallowed hard and whispered a prayer for courage. "Nell, you go on now, when it's time. You know Jesus is coming for you soon," I said, consoling myself. Clearly, I was the one trying to let go of this woman I had come to love so much. "Thank you for everything you have given to me," I said, running my fingers through her short silver hair.

The evening, Frank and I went to Nell's room. Jill and Carolyn, two close friends, came along with us. We entered the hospital room, happy to see Nell awake. With friends gathered around her bedside, she was her usual, spunky self. Passing out bright smiles from underneath the oxygen mask, Nell seemed determined to go out in style, just as she had lived—vibrant, vulnerable, trusting.

As we all talked, a tall, gorgeous middle-aged lady walked in and gave us all a greeting. Rushing to the bedside, she bent to kiss her mother. It was Janet, who had just arrived from Chicago. "Wow, you have a beautiful daughter," Carolyn said, admiring Nell's attractive, fifty-ish offspring. Bright-eyed, Nell managed to raise her brows and point to herself as if to say, *Well, sure! She belongs to me!* A round of laughter echoed off the walls of the hospital room. Michael and David, her sons, also arrived. We made a bit of small talk, and then the room grew silent.

The family members hadn't seen Nell for quite some time, so I decided to break the ice. "Well, Nell, I guess I'll have to write some more about you. You know why?" I asked her. She raised her eyebrows.

Why? she asked with her eyes.

"Because now you're like the Velveteen Rabbit—getting ready to step into Real. Just waiting for Jesus to come for you." Tonight, Nell was letting go of the life she had known and loved, and the people she had given so much to.

Yes, she nodded her head and smiled. With the joy of a five year old about to take her first ride on a Ferris wheel—a tiny bit of fear of the unknown mixed with an overwhelming sense of excitement and anticipation for what was to come—Nell smiled broadly from underneath the oxygen mask. As she did, her entire face took on a childlike glow. Although she couldn't talk or even write us a note, Nell could still nod her head, and those eyes of hers could twinkle as brightly

At Last!
At Last!

as ever. Every patch of fur—all of it—had been rubbed off. Nell's Real skin was now exposed as she lay in her bed, waiting. Eager to answer God's whisper calling her home.

ARISE, SHINE;
FOR YOUR LIGHT HAS COME!
AND THE GLORY OF THE LORD IS
RISEN UPON YOU.

ISAIAH 60:1 (NKJV)

The next morning, Saturday, Nell's other daughter, Diane, arrived and visited with her mother. Perhaps it had been this last farewell to her oldest daughter that kept Nell hanging on. That afternoon the family met in the hospital lobby to share memories of favorite moments with Nell.

"In some ways, I have felt like I was in your place," I said to Janet and Diane. "Sort of like standing on stolen ground, getting to live near Nell and all."

"Oh, we're so glad you were here with her," Janet responded graciously. "We couldn't be, and it's so nice that she had you."

"Brenda, thanks for opening up the conversation about death," David said. "I wanted to talk to her about going on to heaven, but I didn't know where to start. You made it easy."

"*The Velveteen Rabbit* made it easy," Michael clarified. And then came a very pleasant surprise I didn't deserve. "You're just the right age to be Mom's daughter," Michael said.

"Yeah, and you're tall like Janet and Diane too," David chimed in.

"You're an honorary Tamillow," Diane pronounced.

"Oh, no," I protested, recalling the many times Nell wanted to visit with me, and I hadn't made the time for her. But I was outnumbered. And my guilty conscience was no match for their grace.

"Yes. An honorary Tamillow," they echoed in unison.

"Thank you," I finally agreed, tearfully.

The next morning, Sunday, Nell died peacefully, in her sleep.

The Bride of Christ

For your Maker is your husband,
the Lord of hosts is His name.

Isaiah 54:5 (nkjv)

Nell was a remarkable woman. A Real woman. She was witty, elegant, wild-spirited, intoxicated with life, and strangely careless about death. She was a bundle of paradoxes, gulping life to the last drop like a glass of cool water, yet eager to drink the cup of death when her summons came. I would miss Nell for a long, long time. Knowing she had gone on to heaven ahead of me had a way of raising my anticipation for the day I would pass through the veil of this life, into the arms of Jesus.

A few days after her passing, I was in the bookstore picking up a couple of books I had special ordered. One of them caught the clerk's eye as she rang up my purchases. *"The Sacred Romance,"* she mused aloud, looking at the cover. "Now that sounds interesting."

"I really liked it, and I'm buying this copy for a friend," I said.

"You know," the clerk said slowly, somewhat reluctantly, "my husband died last year and sometimes I am so lonely." I nodded in sympathy, then she went on. " I know the Bible says that as Christians we are the bride of Christ. But *how* are we the bride of Christ?" We made a bit more small talk and I left the store, but the clerk's question haunted me.

How are we the bride of Christ?

The following weekend I would see the movie *Ever After,* which is based on the fairy tale *Cinderella.* In the opening scenes of the movie, a young girl named Danielle is enjoying the company of her father, who loves her very much. With her mother now deceased, Danielle shares favorite games and rituals, and special kinds of good-night kisses with

196

her father exclusively. She goes to sleep each night listening to the sound of his voice reading her favorite stories. Each time Danielle's father leaves for a business trip, he stops his horse, turns, and waves when he gets to the gate—it's tradition. Danielle wouldn't think of going inside before watching her beloved father wave good-bye and ride away. All their small rituals have deep significance and foster her security.

At Last! At Last!

Until, one day, Danielle's father falls from his horse and dies before he gets to the gate. Danielle is heartbroken. The traditional fairy tale follows. Danielle lives out her Cinderella life with a wicked step-mother and two devious stepsisters. But even with her cinder-smeared face and servant's clothing, Danielle's sense of bold adventure and courage cannot be hidden. As fairy tale fate would have it, Prince Henry falls in love with Danielle—a commoner—and she becomes his bride. Danielle is his perfect match. Through the trials of life, Danielle had never lost her hope for finding true love. The movie ends as the couple is married and begins their "happily ever after" life together.

The bookstore clerk's question lingered in my mind after the movie was over, intermingling with scenes from *Ever After,* and inspiring thoughts of a Real love story—a true story of a woman's courtship with Jesus. While Nell had gone on to heaven and now understood from God's own perspective what it means to be the bride of Christ, the widowed bookstore clerk could only guess what it will be like on that day. *Perhaps,* I thought, *if she could somehow completely understand today, the love story leading up to her future wedding day with Christ* (and if you and I could, too), *it might go something like this:*

Once upon a time there lived a woman named ____ (fill in your name). From the first moment she first lay quietly nestled in her mother's womb, Jesus saw her, and He loved her very much. She was His beloved. During all her little-girl days, Jesus watched over the child, sending ribbons of sunshine during her days and guardian angels to dance around her bed through the night. He whispered His love to her as she played in the raspberry canes, and they had rides in the wheelbarrow together. They spent long days together playing their favorite games and enjoying many family traditions. Theirs was a life of simple abundance. The girl went to sleep each night to the sound of Jesus' voice as He read to her from His book. She would rather hear His voice than any other sound.

As the girl grew into a young adult, her Beloved often seemed distant, and she sometimes doubted His love. His Voice grew faint. Although He promised to return for her when the time was right, the image of His face dimmed in her mind. Days and years passed and she grew into a woman. The woman grew weary from life's catastrophes, and she never knew just how hard Jesus worked to smooth out the roughest edges from her days. Family and friends would come and go, dreams would die, and new hopes would be born.

The Velveteen Woman

It pained Jesus greatly that the woman could not always see Him, hear Him, feel His longing for her—a longing deeper than any she could possibly imagine. More than anything, He wanted her to grow and mature as His beautiful bride. Somehow, throughout even the most devastating losses of life, the woman never lost hope of her union with Him. Someday, she would be His bride.

As the woman grew into old age, she lay on her deathbed, reflecting on her earthly days with Jesus, her First Love. It had not been an easy life. Her face was now etched with pain. But to Jesus, she was always beautiful. She was His bride—His perfect match. And tomorrow, on their wedding day, she would see Him fact to face. From that moment on, they would be together forever and ever, and live happily ever after.

THE END

IT IS THE UNION WITH GOD THAT IS THE ORIGINAL,
AND THE HUMAN UNION THAT IS THE IMITATION, JUST
AS THE MARITAL UNION OF ADAM AND EVE WAS AN
IMAGE OF THE CREATIVE ACT WHEREBY GOD CREATED
EACH ONE OF THEM, BODY AND SOUL, AND CREATED
THEM IN RELATIONSHIP TO HIMSELF.[1]

MAXIMILIAN MARNAU

Even in life's pinnacle success stories, boldest adventures, and happiest marriages, there is a sense of incompleteness, a longing for more. We want our First Love, and this is as it should be. St. Augustine expressed this longing so well: "Thou hast made us for Thyself, and our hearts are restless till they rest in Thee."[2] Healthy marriages have a mystical way of revealing God—a way of bringing moments of peace to restless hearts. But relief is temporary. The feeling of incompleteness remains. To become totally Real, we have to wait until we see Jesus face to face.

One of the most compelling love stories in our time involves a couple who, in the beginning, lived an ocean apart. He was a Christian apologist, Oxford bachelor, and author of children's books. She was an American woman, divorced with two sons. C.S. Lewis and Joy Davidman met during her visit to England in 1952. At first, they cor-

At Last!
At Last!

responded by mail, nourishing their relationship with stimulating, intellectual letters. Joy moved to England with her boys. When her lack of funds and an expiring visitor's visa threatened Joy's departure from England, C.S. Lewis made a decision to marry her, if she would agree. She did. But early in their marriage, an irreversible form of cancer was discovered in Joy's body. Into the well-ordered life of C.S. Lewis, confusion and uncertainty were introduced. But in the process, he realized how deeply he loved Joy.

The couple obtained the blessing of the church on their marriage. Joy was given the best medical treatment available in the hospital, and then C.S. Lewis brought her home to care for her personally. Joy's body responded with a brief remission.

"You have made me happy," Joy told him, just before she died. "She smiled," Lewis later recalled, "but not at me."[3] Even in this most amazing love story with passionate spiritual depth, the couple's oneness was not complete. Joy died with the smile of anticipation on her face—anticipation of becoming Real when she'd be united with her First Love.

What will it be like to see Jesus face to face? To be like Him? To be completely Real? Nell once told me that she imagined herself arriving on heaven's shores riding up to Jesus on a white stallion, long silver hair flowing behind her head. Her words echo in my mind: "Jesus is there on the beach, waiting for me, welcoming me home with a smile that says, 'At last, we are together, My love!' As the waves lap around the hooves of His high-spirited steed, Jesus reaches out for me. I take His hand and gracefully slither my heavenly, pain-free body onto the back of His horse, taking my place as His bride. Then we ride off into the sunset together."

At times, I have pictured my own homegoing something like the end of the epic movie *Titanic*, when Rose imagines her final meeting with Jack. In my mind's eye, as I approach the red-carpeted staircase, all the people I have loved who have gone on before me line the hallway—my dad, my mom, and grandparents. Nell and little Scotty Windsor are there too. I am so happy to see them but there is no time for greetings. For there at the top of the staircase, in the finest white tuxedo stands Jesus, smiling. Waiting for me.

At last! At last!

What will it be like in heaven? We have only bits and pieces of information in His Word. Most of it is left to mystery, strange and wonderful, like nursery magic. Who are you looking forward to seeing at your homegoing? How do you picture heaven? Has your life been so filled with disappointments and tears that you've struggled to hang onto hope? This is the one thing we must never lose—hope in God.

AND HOPE DOES NOT DISAPPOINT US, BECAUSE GOD HAS POURED OUT
HIS LOVE INTO OUR HEARTS BY THE
HOLY SPIRIT, WHOM HE HAS GIVEN US.

ROMANS 5:5

Becoming Real

As I close this last chapter, I am reminded of a woman I will call Cassie. A friend who often struggled in her life with God, who had frequent bouts of depression and, for the most part, felt unworthy of God's love. One day as we sat together at my kitchen table, she told me this story:

"When I was a little girl, my parents kept a Bible in our living room. It sat on the coffee table, and nobody talked about it. The big, mysterious book was just there." Suddenly, Cassie's eyes glazed over, and I knew a part of her had gone back to that time in her life, to that familiar living room. "I wanted to read the Bible, so my mom let me take it into my bedroom. But nobody explained it to me. I opened the big, unmanageable book, but I could not read. I didn't know what it said.

"Then I started going to Sunday School and learning about God and His love for me. Years passed. In late adolescence, well, you know what happened," Cassie lowered her voice and her head as she recalled years of sexual abuse she'd previously confided to me.

"Yes. I know, Cassie," I said, reaching to touch my friend's hand.

"I could not figure out why God would say He loved me," she continued, "when He had let those horrible things happen to me. I raged at Him. I was disappointed when Christian friends let me down, as well. But somehow, through it all, I still wanted God. Even when I was mad at Him, I wanted more of Him."

At Last!
At Last!

Cassie stopped to clear her throat, now fixing her eyes intently on mine. "What will make Him Real for me?" she asked. "For *me*." As we sat in silence, we both knew the answer was beyond us. But just then, an unsolicited thought popped into my mind. It was one of those rare moments I have only experienced a few times in my whole life, when a wispy puff of truth seemed to present itself, almost super naturally.

"He will," came the words. "*He* will make Himself Real for you, as He has already been doing, little by little." As I looked into Cassie's eyes, we both understood that somehow, mysteriously, we were hearing these words together. "Don't you see?" I continued. "God has been calling to you all through the years, as you have just explained to me. Now, you are very Real to God because He loves you. But one day, He will be completely Real to you, just as you are to Him. It's been happening gradually, a little at a time, even though you haven't been aware of it."

"But what can *I do* to become more Real? To make Him more Real to me?" Cassie asked.

"Just keep believing, and keep following your longing for Him. Listen for His voice, and don't give up hope. "

"But I thought I would come to a point where I would not feel so lonely anymore. I thought I would feel brave and strong as I matured spiritually," she said.

"Ah yes, we all want that, and it will come one day," I said, gently squeezing Cassie's hand. "But not now. Not in this life. This life is not a fairy tale, but it does end like one."

IF I FIND IN MYSELF DESIRES NOTHING IN THIS WORLD CAN
SATISFY, THE ONLY LOGICAL EXPLANATION IS THAT
I WAS MADE FOR ANOTHER WORLD.[4]

C.S. LEWIS

It is especially for women like Cassie that *The Velveteen Woman* has been written. For those who struggle, who suffer, who have become discouraged and confused about what it means to be loved by God. For those who anxiously wonder, *What can I do to become Real?* For those who long for Jesus, and have tried hard to live for Him, looked everywhere for His love.

The Velveteen Woman

I, too, am a Velveteen Woman. As you know by now, I have been down lots of rabbit trails only to find detours, roadblocks and deadends. Somehow I found my way back to the path. Because God was the One who loved me, who called to me, whispering messages of His love. I just had to learn to stop, look, and listen. He was there in my own backyard, painting a glorious sunset across the horizon especially for me. There in the soothing sound of the poplar leaves, shaking gently as the breeze passed by in soft caresses. There in my own home, written down in a big book on the coffee table. There in my own heart.

We will have moments of good life, yes. But only moments. If Christ Himself experienced the agony of separation from His Father, is it reasonable to think we won't? We are the bride of Christ, but our wedding day has not yet come. To become totally Real, and to know our First Love with skin on, we must wait. In the meantime, we can take turns sharing bits of truth with each other, telling how we are finding nuggets of God's love scattered here and there along the path. None of us has all the answers. On some days, we play the part of the wise Skin Horse, at other times we are the vulnerable, frightened Velveteen Rabbit.

Stop. Look around you. Listen for His voice. Becoming Real is a thing that happens to you, perhaps while you're not even noticing. While you're busy getting shabbier and shabbier, having all your fake fur rubbed off by the abrasions of everyday life. All the while, God has been loving you. Holding you close to His heart, carrying you with Him everywhere He goes, whispering to you. Yes, He has been loving you—REALLY loving you—for a long, long time.

Fake Fur Perception:

Because I am the bride of Christ, I should feel complete now.
I can become totally Real here on earth.

Real Skin Reality:

I am the bride of Christ. Until that time when I see Him face to face
with skin on—when I become completely Real—
I will have an unsatiable longing for union with Jesus.

Notes

CHAPTER TWO

1. Louisa Fletcher, *The Land of Beginning Again* (Boston: Small, Maynard & Company, 1921), p. 6.
2. Brennan Manning, *The Ragamuffin Gospel* (Sisters, OR: Multnomah Books, 1990), p. 168.
3. A.W. Tozer, *The Pursuit of God* (Harrisburg, PA: Christian Publications, 1943), p. 34.
4. Manning, p. 53.
5. Billy Graham, quoted by Eugene H. Peterson in *The Message* (Colorado Springs: NavPress, 1995), p. 63.
6. Philip Yancey, *What's So Amazing About Grace?* (Grand Rapids, MI: Zondervan, 1997), p. 195.
7. Friends in Recovery with Jerry S., *The Twelve Steps — A Spiritual Journey* (San Diego: Recovery Publications, 1993), p. 56.

CHAPTER THREE

1. Albert Nolan, *Jesus Before Christianity* (Maryknoll, New York: Orbis Books, 1997), p. 45.
2. Richard Selzer, M.D., *Mortal Lessons: Notes on the Art of Surgery* (New York: Simon and Schuster, 1978), pp. 45-46. I shortened an account of this story I saw in *The Ragamuffin Gospel*, pp. 105-106.

CHAPTER FOUR

1. Roy and Revell Hession, *We Would See Jesus* (Fort Washington, PA: Christian Literature, 1958), p. 15.
2. John Powell, *Why Am I Afraid To Tell You Who I Am?* (Allen, TX: Thomas More, 1969), p. 65.
3. Kathleen Norris, *Amazing Grace* (New York: Riverhead Books, 1998), p. 57.
4. Dan Allender and Tremper Longman III, *Cry of the Soul* (Colorado Springs: NavPress, 1994) p. 125. I highly recommend this book for gaining understanding of how the psalms expose the nature of our emotional responses to God.
5. Sue Monk Kidd, *When the Heart Waits* (San Francisco: Harper, 1990), p. 8.
6. Don Hudson, "Searching For Our Fathers," in *Mars Hill Review #10*, (Littleton, CO: Mars Hill Forum, 1998), p. 45.
7. Yancey, p. 206.
8. Scott Peck, *The Road Less Traveled & Beyond* (New York: Simon and Schuster, 1997), p. 75.
9. Brent Curtis and John Eldredge, *The Sacred Romance* (Nashville, TN: Thomas Nelson, 1997), p. 174. This book vividly describes the longings of the the the heart to commune with God, and ways we kill desire to avoid pain. I recommend it highly.
10. Michael J. Kendall's poem in Dorothy C. Brigg's *Embracing Life*, (New York: Doubleday, 1985), p. 124.

Chapter Five

1. Steve Brown, *Approaching God—How to Pray* (Nashville, TN: Moorings Press, 1996), p. 74.
2. Henri Nouwen in a public address entitled "Living as the Beloved" at Church of the Ressurection, Dallas, TX, 1993.
3. Nolan, p. 48.
4. Peterson, Matthew 7:1.
5. Peterson, John 8:7.

Chapter Six

1. Curtis and Eldredge, p. 164.
2. C.S. Lewis, *Perelandra* (New York: Collier Books, 1944), p. 64.
3. Curtis and Eldredge, p. 151.
4. Quote from Henri Nouwen in a public address in Dallas, TX, 1993.
5. Margo Maine, *Father Hunger* (Carlsbad, CA: Gurze Books, 1991).
6. Debra Evans, *Beauty and the Best,* (Colorado Springs: Focus on the Family, 1993), p. 137.

Chapter Seven

1. Amy Tan quoted by Sarah Ban Breathnach in *Simple Abundance* (New York: Warner Books, 1995), March 14.
2. John Powell, *Why Am I Afraid To Love?* (Allen, TX: Argus Communications, 1967), p. 24.
3. Gilda Radner quoted by Lee Ezell in *Will the Real Me Please Stand Up!* (Nashville, TN, Thomas Nelson, 1995), p. 55.

Chapter Eight

1. Shel Silverstein, *The Giving Tree* (New York: Harper and Row, 1964).
2. Elisabeth Elliot, *Loneliness* (Nashville, TN: Thomas Nelson, 1988), p. 148.
3. Peck, p. 60.
4. Thomas Merton, quoted in Manning, p. 22.

Chapter Nine

1. Gary Chapman, *The Five Love Languages* (Chicago: Northfield Publishing, 1992), p. 15.
2. Ken Gire, *Windows of the Soul,* (Grand Rapids, MI: Zondervan, 1996), front jacket.
3. Oswald Chambers quoted by Curtis and Eldredge, audiotape (Nashville, TN: Thomas Nelson, 1997).
4. Max Lucado, *Just in Case You Ever Wonder* (Dallas: Word Publishing, 1992).
5. Luci Shaw, "Art and Christian Spirituality: Companions in the Way" in *Mars Hill Review #10* (Littleton, CO: Mars Hill Forum, 1998) p. 27.

Chapter Ten

1. Powell, *Why Am I Afraid To Love?,* p. 151.
2. Peterson, *The Message,* p. 58.
3. Ibid.

4. Joseph Bayly, "Mojave Desert," *Psalms of My Life* (Colorado Springs: Chariot Victor Publishing, 1987), p. 76.
5. Isaiah 52:14.
6. Amy Carmichael, *Rose from Brier* (Fort Washington, PA: Christian Literature Crusade, 1977), p. 50.

CHAPTER ELEVEN

1. Luke 10:26-28
2. Hession, p. 5.
3. St. Augustine, *Confessions 10*, quoted by David Hazard in *Early Will I Seek You* (Minneapolis: Bethany House, 1991), p. 18.
4. Amy Carmichael, *Toward Jerusalem* (Fort Washington, PA: 1977), p. 83.
5. Annie Dillard, *Pilgrim at Tinker Creek* (New York: Harper Collins, 1974) p. 4.
6. Henri Nouwen, *Life of the Beloved* (New York, NY: Crossroads Publishing, 1992), p. 82-83.

CHAPTER TWELVE

1. Kidd, p. 48.
2. Psalm 42:1
3. Psalm 139:7
4. Psalm 139:23
5. J. Keith Miller, *The Secret Life of the Soul* (Nashville, TN).
6. Henri Nouwen, *The Inner Voice of Love* (New York: Doubleday, 1996), p. 8.
7. Quote from Henri Nouwen at a public address in Dallas, TX, 1993.
8. Manning, p. 113.
9. Tony Campollo, *How to Be a Christian Without Embarrassing God* (Dallas: Word Publishing, 1997), audiotape.
10. Psalm 103:14.
11. Manning, p. 183.

CHAPTER THIRTEEN

1. Manning.
2. Lee Ezell, *Will The Real Me Please Stand Up!* (Nashville, TN.: Thomas Nelson, 1995), p. 155.
3. Ibid, p. 154.
4. Charles Spurgeon quoted by Elizabeth Skoglund in *More Than Coping* (Minneapolis: Worldwide Publications, 1979, 1987).
5. Elisabeth Elliot, *Loneliness* (Nashville, TN: Thomas Nelson, 1988), p. 63.
6. Sheila Walsh, *Honestly* (Grand Rapids, MI: Zondervan, 1996), p. 145.
7. Ephesians 2:13

CHAPTER FOURTEEN

1. Rainer Maria Rilke, *Letters to a Young Poet*, trans. M.D. Herter (New York: Norton, 1934), p. 35.
2. Kidd, p. 159.
3. 2 Corinthians 10:5

4. Henri Nouwen, *With Burning Hearts* (New York: Orbis Books, 1996), p. 29.
5. Karen Lawson, personal journal entry, Greenville, TX, 1998.
6. Job 38:4-7
7. Zora Neale Hurston, *Write to the Heart: Wit and Wisdom of Women Writers*, edited by Amber Coverdale Sumrall, (Freedom, CA: The Crossing Press, 1992).
8. Quoted in *The Family Networker 13*, p. 30.
9. Carmichael, "Even as a Weaned Child," *Toward Jerusalem*, p. 92.

CHAPTER FIFTEEN

1. Nouwen, *Life of the Beloved* , p. 76.
2. Ibid., p. 79.
3. C.S. Lewis, *Shadowlands* movie.
4. Nouwen, *With Burning Hearts*, p. 28.
5. Ibid.
6. Matthew 27:46

CHAPTER SIXTEEN

1. Maximilian Marneau, O.S.B., *Gertrude of Helfta: Revelations of Divine Love*, quoted by Kathleen Norris in *The Cloister Walk* (New York, NY: Riverhead Books, 1996), p. 249.
2. St. Augustine, quoted by Curtis and Eldredge, p. 136.
3. Les and Leslie Parrott, *Saving Your Marriage Before It Starts* (Grand Rapids, MI: Zondervan, 1995), p.136.
4. C.S. Lewis, *The Quotable Lewis*, edited by Wayne Martindale and Jerry Root (Wheaton, IL: Tyndale House, 1963), p. 287.